HIGH FENCE FOODIE

From The Big House To Your House

Cooking in prison with Celeste Johnson

High Fence Foodie:
From The Big House To Your House

Published by:
The Justice Institute
PO Box 66291
Seattle, WA 98166
www.justicedenied.org
info@justicedenied.org

First softcover edition, March 2015

ISBN: 0-9855033-3-5
ISBN-13: 978-0-9855033-3-8
LCCN: 2015930246

Special Notes:

TDCJ is the Texas Department of Criminal Justice

Units are Texas Department of Criminal Justice operated prisons

Dedication

Thank you to my mom Nancy Hall, for your unending efforts, dedication, and hard work to support me.

And, to one of my dearest friends, Nathan L. Jordan, Director of "ANGELS" – A Prison Ministry. Simply stated, without you there would be no book. The countless hours you spent typing, proofing, editing and moving text are greatly appreciated. Because of your dedication, generosity, and perseverance, this extremely time-consuming project came to fruition. And, of course you do so much more than all of that for both my mom and me. I don't know what we would do without you. You truly are an "Angel"!

Also, a special thank you to Marcia Kelly for her delicious contributions. Especially, the very creative "Holiday Recipes."

To all my sisters in white who gave me a recipe or two to fill these pages — thank you!

Lastly, to all prisoners who strive to be a better person than the one who entered those gates... Keep your head up and remember that your past does not define you. Every day is a new beginning!

Table of Contents

Preface

Cooking is one of the few ways to express your ingenuity with food products bought at the commissary. Preparing a "spread" in prison is the one thing that is not locked up or trapped by razor wire. A bowl of your own created delicious food becomes a source of liberty and feels more like the free world. Meals in the chow hall are limited to 20 minutes and most are boring and bland. Tuesdays are always "this" and Sundays are always "that". So, whip out the hot pot and select from this fine dining menu – **Mango Bella**!

Happy Cooking!

Celeste

Foodie Pantry

Item	Size		Item	Size
BBQ chips	8 oz		Ketchup	14 oz
BBQ sauce	18 oz		Mackerel	3.5 oz
Beef tips	12 oz		Maria's cookies	40 ea
Cappuccino	.81 oz		Mexican beef	7 oz
Cheese puffs	11 oz		Mustard	12 oz
Chicken chili w/beans	8 oz		Nacho chips	3 oz
Chicken Vienna	6 ea		Onion flakes	1.58 oz
Chili with beans	7.5 oz		Onion powder	2.5 oz
Chili without beans	7.5 oz		Orange slices	18 ea
Chocolate covered peanuts	7 oz		Other cookies	32 ea
Chunk chicken	7 oz		Party mix	11 oz
Coriander seasoning	1.5 oz		Peanut butter	18 oz
Cranberry juice	11.5 oz		Plain potato chips	2 oz
Cream cheese	.75 oz		Pork skins	1.75 oz
Cream cookie	39 ea		Ranch dressing	1.5 oz
Dry instant beans	8 oz		Salad dressing	14 oz
Dry instant chili beans	8 oz		Salsa	15 oz
Dry instant potatoes	4 oz		Salsa Verde chips	6 oz
Dry milk	3.2 oz		Sandwich spread	14 oz
Energizer mix	2.0 oz		Season-All	1.2 oz
Flour tortillas	12 ea		Spam singles	3.0 oz
Garlic powder	2.65 oz		Strawberry preserves	12 oz
Grape jelly	12 oz		Strawberry/Kiwi juice	11.5 oz
Hot chocolate drink mix	32 oz		Summer Sausage	5 oz
Hot fries	1.25 oz		Sunflower seeds	12 oz
Hot sauce	5 oz		Sweet relish	12 oz
Instant oatmeal	1.5 oz		Trail mix	2 oz
Instant rice	8 oz		Tuna	4 oz
Jalapeño cheese	16 oz		V8 juice	11.5 oz
Jalapeño chips	8 oz		Vanilla wafers	16 oz

I

Meals In A Bag

NACHO
CHIPS

Burritos

Basic Soft Tacos

1 bag Dried beans	2 tablespoons Jalapeño cheese
1 package Flour tortillas	Hot sauce (to taste)
2 Jalapeño's (diced)	Black pepper (to taste)
1 bag Pork skins (lightly crushed)	Salsa (to taste)
1 Summer Sausage (diced)	1 cup Corn chips (crushed)

In a large chip bag, add beans, peppers, pork skins, sausage, cheese, hot sauce, and black pepper. Add hot water to cover ingredients, and mix well. Cook in hot pot for about 45 minutes. When ready, remove from hot pot and leave hot pot plugged in (with water in it).

Warm tortillas on top of hot pot, two at a time. Make sure the lid is off. Fill tortillas with meat mixture, sprinkle corn chips on top, salsa (if desired) and more cheese (if desired). Serve with Spanish rice if really hungry!

Serves: 5

VARIATION: You can use 2 packages of chili with or without beans in place of the refried beans. Or, try chicken in place of the sausage. Salsa Verde chips can easily replace the corn chips-just use your imagination!

DID YOU KNOW? Bananas are America's #1 fruit.

Beef Pizza

2 packages Pizza slices	1 package Beef tips
2 packets Cream cheese	2 Jalapeño peppers (sliced)
¼ teaspoon Coriander seasoning	

Drain beef tips. Place in a large bowl and cut beef tips into smaller pieces with edge of spoon. Add cream cheese and seasoning and mix well.

Open pizza slices without tearing package and set the slice on it's package. Top each slice equally with the beef. Top each slice with one of the sliced peppers.

Keep slices on plastic package and slip into a large paper bag (sideways), or a large chip bag or cereal bag (length side). Clip the end almost closed leaving enough room for the nozzle of a blow dryer. Heat on high for a total of 1 hour. After 30 minutes, rotate and turn, switching sides for even cooking.

Enjoy the pizzeria taste!
Serves: 2

DID YOU KNOW? The tomato is in the same family as the potato, pepper, egg plant, and petunia.

Breakfast Bagel

1 Bagel (cut in half)	2 packets Cream cheese
2 teaspoons Strawberry preserves	

Place bagel slices side by side inside a cereal or large chip bag. Heat with blow dryer for about 10 minutes until top is toasted.

Spread 1 packet of cream cheese on each side and top with 1 teaspoon of jam on each side. Enjoy on a Saturday or Sunday with a cup of coffee.

Serves: 1

DID YOU KNOW? Vanilla flavoring is sometimes made with an ingredient from beaver urine.

Burrito Fantastica

3 packages Chili no beans	1 bottle Squeeze cheese
1 bag Dried beans	5 Jalapeño peppers (diced)
2 bags Nacho chips (crushed)	1 can V8 juice
2 packets Chili soup seasonings	1 package Flour tortillas
2 bags Pork skins (crushed)	1 teaspoon Hot sauce
1 bag Cheese puffs (crushed)	Water
1 package Beef tips (drain off gravy)	

Cook dried beans according to package directions, in a large chip bag. Add all the crushed chips, including the pork skins, stir well. Pour in V8 juice. Continue stirring. If needed, add a little water to hydrate chips. You want it to be a little soupy. Cook for 30 minutes.

Add 2/3 bottle of cheese, peppers, hot sauce, seasoning, beef tips (drained), and 2 chili pouches. Mix well. Heat for 30 minutes.

When done, spoon the mixture equally into 12 tortillas. Place 3 burritos into 4 chip bags. Heat for at least 2 hours. Also heat the remaining cheese and chili pouch.

When ready to serve, pour chili over the top of burritos and swirl cheese on top of chili.

Serve with rice and beans. Top cheese with salsa, if desired.

Serves: 4

SUBSTITUTE: 1 bag of Salsa Verde chips can replace the Nacho chips. And, if you like it really hot, try using jalapeño cheese puffs in place of the plain cheese puffs. BBQ beef or 2 packages of the beef stew can be used instead of the beef tips.

DID YOU KNOW? Pumpkins were once recommended for removing freckles and curing snake bites.

Burrito Supreme

3 packages Chili no beans	Salsa (to taste)
2 packages Chili w/beans	2 handfuls Jalapeño chips (crushed)
1 package Mexican meat	1 bag Pork skins (crushed)
1 bag Dried beans	6 Jalapeño peppers
1 package Cheese nips (crushed)	2 packages Flour tortillas
Water	

Cook refried beans according to package directions in a large chip bag. Add pork skins and set aside. Combine the cheese nips and jalapeño chips in a bowl. Add enough water to make the mixture into a paste. Combine the chili with beans and beef with the refined bean mixture. Mix well.

Place a heaping spoonful of cheese mixture on each flour tortilla. Then place a large helping of the bean/beef mixture and roll up the tortillas and place in 5 cooking bags. There will be four in each cooking bag. Heat for 3 hours.

Place all 3 of the chili w/o beans and jalapeños in a large cooking bag and heat. When done, place the burritos in 5 bowls and pour the chili mixture over the top of the burritos.

Serves: 5

VARIATION: Ranch dressing or cream cheese drizzled over the top of the chili mixture tastes good, too. And, when available so does salsa.

DID YOU KNOW? Spotted bananas are sweeter, with a sugar content of more than 20 percent, compared with 3 percent in a green banana.

Celeste's Mackerel Madness

1 package Mackerel	¼ teaspoon Onion powder
4 tablespoons Jalapeño cheese	½ teaspoon Black pepper
1 packet Ranch dressing	¼ bag Tortilla chips
½ teaspoon Garlic powder	6 tablespoons Water

Add all ingredients to your insert cup and stir well. Cook for 45 minutes to 1 hour.
Serve over Tortilla chips. It's quick and tasty!
Serves: 1 (Large portion!)

DID YOU KNOW? Potato plants were grown aboard the space shuttle Columbia in 1995.

Celeste's Special Tuna Nachos

1 package Chili w/beans	1 package Tuna
1 teaspoon Jalapeño chips (crushed)	½ bag Nacho chips
1 packet Ranch dressing	¼ bag Tortilla chips
¼ teaspoon Season-All	Salsa (to taste)
1 Jalapeño pepper (sliced)	¼ bag Salsa Verde chips (whole)
1 teaspoon Salsa Verde chips (crushed)	5 tablespoons Jalapeño cheese

In your insert cup or cooking jar, add tuna, ranch dressing, cheese, crushed chips, and Season-All and mix well. Add hot water, a little at a time, until there is a creamy consistency and continue mixing well. Give the water a chance to absorb into the crushed chips before adding more water. (It usually takes about ⅛ cup of water). Cook in hot pot.

Place the chili pouch in the hot pot standing upright and next to the insert cup. Fill hot pot with water to just underneath the lip. Rest lid on top since it won't properly close because of pouch. (I cover with my cell towel to keep the heat in.) Cook for at least 1 hour. The longer you can cook it the better it will taste. I like it to cook for hours.

When done, place tortilla, Nacho, and Salsa Verde chips inside large bowls. Then pour the chili equally over the top of the chips in each bowl.

Cover the chili with equal amounts of tuna mixture. Pour desired amount of salsa on each. Top with the jalapeños.

These are guaranteed to be the best nachos you have ever tasted. I received an email from a kitchen Captain in the German Air Force requesting this recipe. **Savior!**

Serves: 2 (large portions)

SUBSTITUTE: Mackerel can always be used in place of the tuna. If you use mackerel, you should use 2 packages. Chicken can be used in place of the tuna, too. Chili no beans can replace the chili with beans. Or, you can use refried beans. (I would make the refried beans thin and spicy). **Use your imagination!**

DID YOU KNOW? When a banana is compared to an apple, it has four times the protein, twice the carbohydrates, three times the phosphorus, five times the Vitamin A and Iron, and twice the other vitamins and minerals. It is also rich in potassium and is one of the best food values around.

Cheesy Chicken Nachollas

1 package Chunk chicken	1 Jalapeño pepper (sliced)
¼ bag Cheese puffs (crushed)	¼ bag Tortilla chips
¼ bottle Jalapeño cheese	Salsa (to taste)
4 packets Cream cheese	Water

In a large chip bag, add the crushed cheese puffs, both cheeses, and a little water. Heat and stir and keep adding a little water until creamy.

Then, add chicken and peppers and cook for 45 minutes to 1 hour. When done, pour equally over tortilla chips and top with the desired amount of salsa.

Serves: 2

SUBSTITUTE: You can use Summer Sausage for a "meatier" flavor. Try pouring over Salsa Verde chips instead.

DID YOU KNOW? Americans eat an average of 18 pounds of fresh apples each year. The most popular variety in the United States is the Red Delicious.

Chicken & Chili Nachos

1 bag Tortilla chips	2 packets Ranch dressing
1 bag Dried chili beans	Salsa (if desired)
2 packages Chicken chili	½ bottle Jalapeño cheese
1 Jalapeño pepper (diced)	Water
2 teaspoons Jalapeño chips (crushed)	

In a large chip bag, prepare dried beans according to package directions. You may need to add a little more water so they are creamy and not too thick. Stir in crushed chips. Add the chili, cheese and peppers. Stir well. Cook for about 1 hour.

Divide tortilla chips into 4 bowls and pour mixture on top. Top with salsa, if desired. Swirl even amounts of Ranch dressing on top. **Yummy!**

Serves: 4

SUBSTITUTE: Salsa Verde chips and Nacho chips can easily replace the tortilla chips or use all 3 combined!

DID YOU KNOW? Fortune cookies were actually invented in America in 1918, by Charles Jung, a Los Angeles noodle maker.

Chicken & Dressing

1 package Chunk chicken	4 tablespoons Jalapeño cheese
½ bag Corn chips	3 tablespoons Herb potatoes
2 packets Chicken soup seasoning	2 packets Beef soup seasonings
Water	

Rinse corn chips quickly under water (leaving them in the chip bag) and drain by turning bag over. Then, add ½ cup of water and knead the chips together until it resembles dough. It's easier to do this if you squeeze the sides of the bag.

Add cheese, potatoes, seasonings, and chicken. Mix well. Place in hot pot and cook for 2 hours. I would dump everything into another bag since this bag has been stressed out!

Serves: 2

☺ HELPFUL HINT!! Always double bag your food to prevent leaks into your meal!

DID YOU KNOW? "Little Tongues" is the literal meaning of the Italian word linguine.

Chicken Enchiladas

2 packages Chunk chicken	¼ cup Salsa
1 package Chili no beans	1 package Flour tortillas
2 packets Chicken soup seasoning	2 packets Ranch dressing
1 packet Chili soup seasoning	dash Season-All
1 Jalapeño pepper (diced)	½ bag Corn chips
½ cup Jalapeño chips (crushed)	Water
6 tablespoons Jalapeño cheese	

FILLING: In a large bowl, add chicken, ½ chili no beans, seasonings, (reserve a small amount of the chili), pepper, salsa, 4 tablespoons cheese, chips and stir well. Add a small amount of water to make sure it is not dry. Spoon into 9 tortilla shells and roll up. Place 3 (each) into 3 separate chip bags.

SAUCE: In a bowl, use the other ½ of the chili, 2 tablespoons jalapeño cheese, Ranch dressing, the leftover chili seasoning, and a little water until well blended. Pour over each enchilada in the 3 bags.

Cook for 2 hours. Serve with rice and beans.

Serves: 3

SUBSTITUTE: Substitute the tortilla chips for corn chips and use cream cheese in place of the jalapeño cheese for a milder flavor. Salsa Verde chips make a nice change instead of using the jalapeño chips. And, Nacho chips are good, too!

DID YOU KNOW? The Pillsbury Bake-off has been held every year since 1948.

Chicken Lemon Pepper Rice

1 bag Rice	1 packet Lemon Cool-down
1 Jalapeño pepper (diced)	2 tablespoons Pickle (diced)
1 packet Chicken soup seasoning	1 packet Chili soup seasoning
1 package Chunk chicken	Black pepper to taste
Water	

In a large chip bag, prepare rice according to package directions. Add the remaining ingredients and mix well. Add a little more water (if needed) and mix well. Cook for 1-2 hours.
Serves: 4

SUBSTITUTE: Tuna or mackerel is a good substitute for the chicken (just use 2 packages). If you don't want it spicy, use more pickles in place of the jalapeños.

DID YOU KNOW? The bright orange color of carrots tell you they're an excellent source of Vitamin A, which is important for good eye sight, especially at night. Vitamin A helps your body fight infection, and keeps your skin and hair healthy!

Chicken Nachos

1 Jalapeño pepper (diced)	1 package Chili no beans
1 packet Ranch dressing	½ bag Jalapeño chips (crushed)
1 packet Beef soup seasoning	Jalapeño cheese (desired amount)
Water	1 bag Tortilla chips
2 packages Chunk chicken (cut into smaller cubes)	

In a large chip bag, combine chicken, chili, peppers, chips, seasoning, and desired amount of cheese and mix well. Add a small amount of water for desired consistency.
Cook 1 to 2 hours. Pour over chips and top with cheese and Ranch dressing.
Serves: 4

SUBSTITUTE: Use cream cheese in place of the jalapeño cheese for a milder flavor. Or, add cream cheese in addition to the jalapeño cheese for a creamier texture.

DID YOU KNOW? In Southeast Asia, the banana leaf is used to wrap food (in place of plastic bags and cling wrap), providing a unique flavor and aroma. And, it's environmentally friendly too!

Chicken Nuggets

1 package Chunk chicken (shredded)	2 teaspoons Jalapeño cheese
1 handful BBQ chips (crushed)	½ teaspoon Season-All
1 handful Jalapeño chips (crushed)	1 bag Hot fries (crushed fine)

In a large bowl, add all ingredients, except the Hot fries and BBQ chips. Mix well. In separate bowls, place the Hot fries and BBQ chips.

Mold chicken mixture into nuggets. Then roll in BBQ chips and then Hot fries. Set inside a cereal bag or a large chip bag in a single layer so that sides are not touching. Heat with your blow dryer for total of 45 to 60 minutes. After heating for 20 minutes turn the nuggets over for even cooking. They are done when they are hot and crispy!

Serve with your favorite dipping sauce.

Serves: 2

DID YOU KNOW? An etiquette writer of the 1840's advised, "Ladies may wipe their lips on the tablecloth, but not blow their noses on it."

Chicken Strips

1 package Chunk Chicken	1 bag Plain potato chips (crushed)
½ cup Jalapeño chips (crushed)	2 bags Hot fries (crushed)
½ bag Cheese puffs (crushed)	1 packet Chicken soup seasoning
½ cup Tortilla chips (crushed)	1 packet Chili soup seasoning
1 packet Ranch dressing	Typing paper (torn in strips)

Drain chicken and save juice in a bowl. In a large bowl, mash chicken and add chicken seasoning. Add potato chips, ½ jalapeño chips, and ½ cheese puffs. Stir well and form in 10 to 12 tenders. Set aside.

Coating: Combine tortilla chips, the remaining jalapeño chips, hot fries, and the other ½ of the cheese puffs. Add ½ chili seasoning and mix well. Dip tenders in the juice you saved and roll them in coating mixture. Place each one in a typing paper strip and roll up. Put in cooking bag and cook 1½ to 2 hours. Serve with Ranch as a dip. Or, heat in cereal bag or brown bag with blow dryer for crispy strips.

Serves: 2

VARIATION: You can use BBQ sauce as a dip, too. Ranch dressing mixed with cream cheese makes another good dipping sauce. Or, Ranch dressing mixed with black pepper (lots of it) or mustard with a dab of BBQ sauce. **Use your imagination!**

DID YOU KNOW? January 19 is National Popcorn Day.

Corn Pockets

1 package Chunk chicken	1 bag Pork skins (crushed)
½ bag Corn chips (crushed)	Typing paper (cut in halves)
¼ bag Tortilla chips (crushed)	2 packets Ranch dressing
1 Jalapeño pepper (diced)	3 packets Cream cheese
1 packet Chili soup seasoning	3 tablespoons Salsa
1 packet Beef soup seasoning	¼ bottle Jalapeño cheese
1 packet Chicken soup seasoning	½ bag Rice
½ bag Jalapeño chips (crushed)	

Prepare the rice according to the package directions (using hot water) in a large chip bag. Set aside.

In a large bowl, combine the corn and tortilla chips with chili seasoning. Mix well. Add hot water to dampen enough to spread into squares about 5" by 5". Set dough aside. Tear 6 sheets of typing paper in half and set aside.

In another large bowl, add meat, chicken seasoning, jalapeños, jalapeño chips, pork skins, rice, and cheese. Mix well. You may need to add a small amount of water so it's not dry.

Make dough squares and put one on each ½ sheet of typing paper. Spoon desired amount of meat mixture onto one end of the square. Flatten and fold over and close edges. Place 2 or 3 into separate cooking bags and cook about 2 hours.

Sauce: Mix the Ranch dressing and cream cheese together until there is no lumps. Add the salsa and stir well. Add black pepper (if desired). Pour sauce over pockets and enjoy!

Serves: 4

Crispy Hot Pockets

1 package Chunk chicken (drained well)	1 handful Jalapeño chips (crushed)
1 tablespoon Jalapeño cheese	Water
1 bag Corn chips (crushed)	

Squeeze chicken continuously in the pouch to shred it. Place drained chicken in a chip bag and add cheese and Jalapeño chips. Mix well. Heat in hot pot for 30 minutes.

In another bowl, add corn chips and crush. Add very little water. You want it to form into dough that is not too wet. Split dough in half. On a large chip bag, roll out dough, using your insert cup as a rolling pin. You want the dough to be about 1/4 inch thick.

Place half of the chicken on dough and fold over other half. Seal by pinching dough together. Place inside an empty cereal bag. Repeat with remaining dough and chicken. Make sure the hot pockets don't touch in bag.

Heat with blow dryer for about 20 minutes. Turn each over and cook 10-15 minutes longer until crispy!

Serve with your favorite chips or even potato salad.

Serves: 2

Crisscross Chili Dogs

1 package Chicken Vienna's	1 package Chili no beans
1 Jalapeño pepper (diced)	1 packet Beef soup seasoning
Jalapeño cheese (as desired)	Salad dressing (optional)
Mustard (as desired)	Ketchup (as desired)
6 slices Bread	Jalapeño chips (as desired)

In a chip bag, combine chili, beef seasoning, and jalapeño chips. Add a little water and mix well (this is just to hydrate the chips). Place in hot pot and cook. Leave Vienna's in pouch (to heat) and place beside chip bag and cook both 45 minutes.

Place 1 Vienna on bread, add chili, and top with mustard, cheese, ketchup, and peppers. Just like at a picnic!

Don't forget the potato salad! **Yummy!**

Serves: 3

> **DID YOU KNOW?** McDonald's and Burger King sugar coat their fries so they will turn golden brown.

Desheon's Chicken and Dumplin's

1 package Chunk chicken	1 package Flour tortillas
2 packets Chicken soup seasoning	3 tablespoons Dry milk
Salt and pepper (to taste)	Water

Tear tortillas into pieces and set to the side. In a large chip bag, add the milk and 1½ cups of water and mix well. After milk is dissolved, add the chicken and seasonings and mix well. Cook 45 minutes until hot and steamy. Then, add flour tortillas and cook 5 more minutes. You don't want the tortilla's to get too soft, so watch time. Divide equally into 3 bowls. **Delish!**

Serves: 3

> **DID YOU KNOW?** The largest item on any menu in the world is probably the roast camel. It is sometimes stuffed with a sheep, which is stuffed with chickens, which are stuffed with fish, which are stuffed with eggs.

Enchilada Pie

2 packages Chili no beans	1 bottle Jalapeño cheese
3 Jalapeño peppers (diced)	3 packets Chili soup seasonings
2 packets Beef soup seasonings.	¼ bag Jalapeño chips (crushed)
1 bag Tortilla chips	2 packets Ranch dressing
Water	

In a large cooking bag, combine chili with 1 beef seasoning and ½ chile seasoning. Add jalapeño chips and small amount of hot water (to hydrate chips). Heat in hot pot. Add a little hot water to jalapeño cheese so it's not so thick. Shake well and set aside.

In large bowl, fill ½ with hot water and add 1 beef seasoning and 2-½ chili seasonings and add the tortilla chips. Let set about 1 minute to soak up liquid. You want this to be like a dough.

In another large bowl, alternate tortilla chip mixture then chili, cheese, peppers, and Ranch dressing until the bowl is full. Let set 20 minutes. Then divide into 2 cooking bags and cook about 3 hours. Don't forget to double bag!

Serves: 4

VARIATION: Salsa can be added to the chili mixture for added flavor. Chili with beans can be used in place of the chili no beans for those who like frijoles!

DID YOU KNOW? A family of four could live for ten years off the bread produced by one acre of wheat.

Earla's Chicken Nuggets

1 package Chunk chicken	4 tablespoons Jalapeño cheese
1 handful BBQ chips (crushed)	Salt and pepper (to taste)
1 handful Jalapeño chips (crushed)	1 Jalapeño pepper (chopped fine)
1 packet Chicken soup seasoning	1 bag Hot fries (crushed fine)

In a large bowl, combine everything except the Hot fries. Mix well. Add just enough water to mold the chicken mixture into about 15 nuggets. These will be large.

Crush the Hot fries in the bag. Roll the nuggets in the Hot fries. You can drop them in the bag one at a time, and shake to coat. Place the nuggets inside a cereal bag (length wise and not touching).

Heat for about 30 minutes with a blow dryer on low heat. Turn the nuggets once after 15 minutes, continue heating. Serve with ketchup or your favorite sauce.

Serves: 3

SUBSTITUTE: You can make fish sticks by substituting 2 tuna packages for the chicken. Instead of nuggets, make them about 3 inches long.

Far East Fantasy

1 packet Chili soup seasoning	1 package Fruit & Nut mix (crushed)
2 packages Chunk chicken	1 bag Rice (do not pre-prepare)
½ bottle BBQ sauce	1 packet Lemon-lime sports drink
2 Jalapeño peppers (finely chopped)	1 can Pineapple/Orange juice
1 package Orange slices (cut into small pieces)	

Place one package of jalapeño peppers (chopped) and all of the orange slices in a hot pot insert. Pour BBQ sauce on top of these leaving about 2 inches from the top to allow for stirring. Heat in hot pot. It will take at least 2 hours for the candy to melt. Stir repeatedly.

Pre-heat the can of the pineapple juice in another hot pot. Pull the tab to release the air so it won't explode while heating.

In a large chip bag, mix the dry rice, nuts, remaining peppers, and sports drink together until well blended. Then, pour in the entire can of hot juice. Place bag in hot pot and cook for about an hour until the sauce is done.

In another chip bag, add chicken and coat with some of the BBQ sauce. (Leave the unmelted orange slices inside insert cup and still covered with most of the BBQ sauce.) Heat in another hot pot. When the orange pieces in the sauce have melted, add the sauce to the chicken and place in a large bowl stirring well to coat the meat.

Empty rice into another bowl. Add chili seasoning packet to the rice and stir well to mix everything. Divide the rice equally into serving bowls and top with the orange/chicken mixture.

Serves: 4

☺ **HELPFUL HINT**: The contents are heavy, so it is advisable to double bag everything!

DID YOU KNOW? Van Camp's Pork and Beans were a staple food for Union Soldiers in the Civil War.

Fast and Easy Nachos

1 bag Salsa Verde chips	1 package Mexican meat
½ cup Dried beans (cooked thin)	1 Jalapeño pepper (diced)
½ cup Jalapeño cheese	1 packet Chili soup seasoning
Salsa (optional)	

In a large chip bag place beef, cheese, seasoning, and thinned out beans and stir well. Cook about 45 minutes. Make sure it is well mixed by squeezing the bag many times. You should use a double bag.

When ready, place chips in large bowls and pour over the chips. Top with peppers and more cheese, if desired. Pour salsa on top of peppers, if desired.

Serves: 2

Fish Sandwich

1 package Mackerel	2 tablespoons Salad dressing
¼ bag Pork skins (crushed)	1 tablespoon Jalapeño chips (crushed)
3 tablespoons Jalapeño cheese	1 Jalapeño pepper (diced)
½ packet Chili soup seasoning	4 slices Bread
2 packages Cheese-n-Chive crackers (crushed)	

Drain and rinse mackerel and place in a large bowl. Add all the ingredients and mix well. You may need to add more cheese so that everything sticks together.

Wash your hands first and then form into 2 patties and place on bread that has salad dressing spread on each side.

Serve with your favorite chips or even potato salad.

Serves: 2

SUBSTITUTE: For a milder taste, use cream cheese in place of the jalapeño cheese and use chopped dill pickle in place of the jalapeño pepper. For extra "spice" add chopped "hot" pickle in addition to the jalapeño pepper.

DID YOU KNOW? During the Alaskan Klondike gold rush (1897-1898) potatoes were practically worth their weight in gold. Potatoes were so valued for their Vitamin C content that miners traded gold for potatoes.

Frito Bandito Pie

1 package Chili w/beans	3 tablespoons Jalapeño cheese
1 Jalapeño pepper (diced)	½ bag Dried beans
½ bag Corn chips	Water

Open the top of the chili pouch and place in hot pot. Into the chili pouch, add 3 tablespoons of water and a long squirt of cheese. Mix well and let cook about 45 minutes.

Then, place the dried beans in a large chip bag and add water according to package directions. Add the chili to this and mix well. Cook about 30 minutes. Pour over the top of corn chips. Top with jalapeños. Pretend you're at the racetrack and enjoy!

Serves: 2

DID YOU KNOW: Vitamin A is known to prevent "night blindness," and carrots are loaded with Vitamin A. One carrot provides more that 200% of the recommended daily intake of Vitamin A. A health bonus is carrots have 0 fat content.

Gumbo Special

1 package Chunk chicken	½ bag Jalapeño chips (crushed)
1 Summer Sausage	2 bags Hot fries (crushed)
1 package Beef stew	1 Jalapeño pepper (diced)
1 bag Rice	¼ Pickle (diced)
1 packet Chicken soup seasoning	1 packet Chili soup seasoning

In a large cooking bag, mix everything together, except for the rice. Cook at least 2 hours. Don't forget to double bag!

In another large cooking bag, prepare rice according to package directions. When done, divide rice evenly into 5 bowls. Pour gumbo over the rice.

Serve with your favorite crackers or chips.

Serves: 5

DID YOU KNOW? Celery has negative calories. It takes more calories to eat a piece of celery than the celery has in it to begin with.

Gumbolicious

1 package Stew meat (mashed in pouch)	¼ bag Salsa Verde chips (crushed)
1 package Mackerel (made into flakes)	¼ bag Pork skins (crushed)
1 Summer Sausage (chopped)	¼ bag Jalapeño chips (crushed)
dash Hot sauce	1 bag Hot fries (crushed)
Water	

Place first 4 ingredients in a large bowl and combine. Divide chips into two empty cooking bags and add equal amounts of mixture and just enough water to hydrate chips. Heat in hot pot for 2 hours. Serve over rice or with your favorite crackers.

Serves: 2

SUBSTITUTE: Tuna is always a good replacement for the mackerel. 2 Spam singles can be used in place of the Summer Sausage since the sausage is a seasonal item.

☺ **HELPFUL HINT**: Double bag each so that you do not have a problem with the bag tearing when removing from your hot pot.

DID YOU KNOW? The FDA allows an average of 30 or more insect fragments, and one or more rodent hairs, per 100 grams of peanut butter. I will certainly think twice before buying my next jar.

Hot Jalapeño Bombers

12 Jalapeño peppers	1 package Mexican meat
½ cup Corn chips (crushed fine)	2 tablespoons Salsa
6 packets Cream cheese	2 packets Chili soup seasoning
¼ bag Rice	½ cup Jalapeño chips (crushed fine)
Typing paper torn in strips	

Cook rice in a large chip bag, according to package directions and set aside.

Clean the core out of the peppers from the stem end to hollow out the pepper. Leave the peppers whole (to stuff).

In a large bowl, mix 4 packets of the cream cheese together with the rice, beef, salsa, and one of the chili seasonings. Mix well making sure everything is blended. Then, fold in the crushed jalapeño chips. Stuff this mixture into the hollowed out pepper.

In another large bowl, combine the remaining seasoning packet with the crushed corn chips. Coat the peppers with the last 2 cream cheese packets and roll in corn chip mixture. Wrap each pepper individually in paper and place in cooking bag.

Heat for about 2 hours.

Serves: 6

☺ HELPFUL HINT: This was too much work to not double-bag!

DID YOU KNOW? China uses 45 billion chopsticks per year. 25 million trees are chopped down to make them.

It's Christen's Favorite

1 package Tuna	1 handful BBQ chips (crushed)
6 Flour tortilla's	1 handful Jalapeño chips (crushed)
½ bag Rice	½ cup Jalapeño cheese
¼ bag Dried beans	¼ teaspoon Garlic powder
1 packet Chile soup seasoning	Water (about an insert cupful)

In a large bowl, combine the tuna with the chili seasoning and garlic powder. Mix well.

Then, add the rice and mix well. Next, add the beans and mix well. Add the cheese and chips stirring well. Finally, add just enough water to hydrate everything. You want it to be creamy not soupy.

Spoon into 6 tortillas and place 3 each in 2 chip bags. Cook for 1 hour.

Serves: 2

DID YOU KNOW? A cluster of bananas is called a hand and consists of 10-20 bananas known as fingers.

Jessica's Special Chili Dogs

1 package Chili no beans	1 Jalapeño pepper (chopped)
1 package Chicken Vienna's	2 teaspoons Pickle (chopped)
6 slices Bread	4 tablespoons Jalapeño cheese
1 cup Corn chips	Hot sauce (to taste)
4 teaspoons Salad dressing	

Pour jalapeño cheese in an insert cup to heat and place in hot pot. Heat Vienna's and chili alongside of cheese (leave in pouches) for about 30 minutes.

Spread about ½ teaspoon of salad dressing on each slice of bread and place 3 in each bowl. Cut Vienna's lengthwise and place 2 halves on each slice of bread (so, they overlay in middle). Pour the chili over the Vienna's and bread. Divide it equally between the bowls. (You want it to cover everything because these are eaten with a spoon and not your hands).

Sprinkle the corn chips on top of this. Then spoon cheese on top. The peppers and pickles are next. Drizzle the desired amount of hot sauce over everything.

Serves: 2

SUBSTITUTE: Chili with beans can always be used and also mustard or ketchup. Sandwich spread can easily replace the salad dressing.

> **DID YOU KNOW?** Darker green lettuce leaves are more nutritious than lighter green leaves.

Laura and Nina's Weekend Special

1 package Chunk chicken	2 tablespoons Salad dressing
1 Summer Sausage (cut in cubes)	½ bag Rice
2 packets Ranch dressing	4 tablespoons Jalapeño cheese
2 packets Cream cheese	Water
1 Jalapeño pepper (diced)	

Place everything (except for rice) into a large chip bag and mix well. Heat in hot pot for at least 2 hours. The longer you cook the better it will taste.

When you are ready to eat, prepare the rice according to package directions. When rice is done, divide into 2 large bowls and pour the chicken/sausage over the rice.

This is quick, easy and absolutely delicious!

Serves: 2

> **DID YOU KNOW?** It takes about a half-gallon of water to cook macaroni, and about a gallon of water to clean the pot.

Laura's Mackerel Lemon/Rice

½ bag Rice	1 packet Lemon Cool-down
1 handful Jalapeño chips (crushed)	1 package Mackerel
¼ Pickle (diced)	Water

In a large chip bag, cook rice according to package directions. Then, add the chips, pickle, and Cool-down and mix well. Heat mackerel alongside the rice mixture (leave in pouch). When the rice is done and the mackerel is hot, fold (don't stir) the mackerel into the rice. Serve with your favorite chips.

Serves: 2

SUBSTITUTE: Tuna can be used in place of the mackerel. The Cool-down can be replaced with a lemon lime sports drink if necessary.

DID YOU KNOW? Truffles or mushrooms that grow below the ground, are one of the world's most expensive foods. One variety, *melanesporum* can cost between $800 and $1,500 a pound.

LeeAnn's Crabby Patties

1 package Tuna	3 tablespoons Jalapeño cheese
6 Croissants	1 packet Chili seasoning
1 Jalapeño pepper (diced)	dash Salt
1 packet Ranch dressing	dash Pepper

In a large bowl, mix all ingredients together (except the croissants). Make sure everything is well blended.

Cut each croissant ¾ of the way lengthwise as if you were making a sandwich. Place two heaping spoonfuls of mixture into each.

Set on paper and place in a paper bag. Heat with blow dryer for one hour. Rotate during heating so all are evenly cooked.

These will amaze you – they taste like crab cakes!

Serves: 2

DID YOU KNOW? The recipe for hamburger pie, which has been updated and republished a number of times over the years, was first published 50 years ago. It has been requested most frequently through the years by the readers of "Better Homes and Gardens."

Mac and Cheesy Spam

2 Spam singles (cut in cubes)	½ cup Jalapeño cheese
1 package Ramen chicken soup	¼ cup Salad dressing
½ sleeve Saltine crackers	Salt & Pepper (to taste)
1 Jalapeño pepper (remove seeds and dice)	Water

Cook soup according to package directions. Drain and pour into a large chip bag. Add all ingredients (except crackers). Mix well. Cook in hot pot for about 1 hour. Divide equally into 2 large bowls and serve with crackers.

Serves: 2

SUBSTITUTE: Chicken can easily be used in place of the Spam singles. And, crushed Cheese Nips taste good sprinkled on top after it's in the bowls.

DID YOU KNOW? Cheese closes the stomach and should always be served at the end of the meal.

Marcia's Stuffed Peppers

½ cup Nacho chips (crushed)	1 package Tuna
¼ cup Rice (cooked)	1 packet Ranch dressing
2 tablespoons Jalapeño cheese	4 packets Cream cheese
1 packet Chicken soup seasoning	1 packet Chili soup seasoning
1 cup Cheese puffs (crushed)	¼ cup Jalapeño chips (crushed)
1 bag Hot fries (crushed)	Water
10 Jalapeño peppers (seeded and cut in half)	

Coating: Combine Nacho chips, ½ of the jalapeño chips, hot fries and a few cheese puffs. Add chili seasonings. Stir well and set aside.

In another large bowl, combine tuna, rice, cheese, Ranch dressing, ½ of the jalapeño chips, and chicken seasoning. Stir well and set aside.

In another large bowl, mix cream cheese, water and enough cheese puffs to make a thick paste and set aside. Stuff tuna mixture in jalapeño pepper to cover the bottom of the pepper then roll in cheese paste. Then roll in chip coating and put in a cooking bag.

Cook 45 minutes to 1 hour. Serve with your favorite dipping sauce.

Serves: 2

DID YOU KNOW? The world's oldest known recipe is for beer.

Meaty Rice Casserole

1 bag Rice	1 package Chili no beans
1 bag Pork skins (crushed)	2 Jalapeño peppers (sliced)
½ bag Jalapeño chips (crushed)	1 package Chicken Vienna's (sliced)
2 bags Hot fries (crushed)	4 tablespoons Jalapeño cheese
1 package Mexican meat	Water
2 packets Soup seasoning (any flavor)	

In a large bowl, prepare rice according to the package directions adding the seasoning packets. Cover with hot water and stir. Let sit for about 45 minutes covered with your cell towel to keep heat in. Crush chips and set aside.

Heat in hot pot (leaving in their pouches) the chili, meat, and Vienna's while waiting for rice. (Slice Vienna's before cooking).

Slice Jalapeño's and add to rice after its done. Then, add the crushed chips and the heated pouches. Stir in cheese and mix well.

Serve with your favorite crackers or chips.

Serves: 4

SUBSTITUTE: Try using 2 Spam singles instead of the Vienna's for a different flavor. And, if you want a "sweeter" flavor, use BBQ chips in place of the jalapeño chips. Don't forget the hot sauce, too!

DID YOU KNOW? Brazil nuts are only grown in rain forests.

Mexically Chicken Tacos

1 package Chunk chicken	1 packet Chicken soup seasoning
½ bag Corn chips (crushed)	1 packet Chili soup seasoning
¼ bag Jalapeño chips (crushed)	1 Jalapeño pepper (diced)
6 Flour tortillas	2 packets Ranch dressing
4 tablespoons Jalapeño cheese	Salsa (to taste)

In a large bowl, combine all ingredients, except the salsa and flour tortillas. Mix well and then spoon mixture equally into 6 flour tortillas. If desired, add salsa before closing tortilla.

Place 3 tacos (each) into 2 large cooking bags and cook in hot pot for about 2 hours. Make sure your tacos face the same way so you don't have a mess!

Serve with a side of rice or beans.

Serves: 2

DID YOU KNOW? An egg will float if placed in water in which sugar has been added.

Philadelphia Cheese Steak Bagel

2 Bagels	1 package Beef tips
1 handful BBQ chips (crushed)	4 tablespoons Jalapeño cheese
2 packets Cream cheese	

Slice bagel in half. Drain liquid off beef tips and place beef tips in a large bowl. Add the chips and cheese and mix well.

With the handle of the spoon, hollow out the dough from each bagel slice. (Eat as a snack). Fill bagel with your meat mixture and place together (like a sandwich). It will be very fat!

Place a whole bagel in a coffee, milk, or chunk chicken bag, because the foil in these bags allow the bagel to get a little crispy. Cook for 1 hour.

This will be your new fave!

Serves: 2

SUBSTITUTE: Summer Sausage, 2 Spam singles, or Chicken taste equally good!

DID YOU KNOW? The average French citizen eats 500 snails per year.

Pizza Pocket

2 packages Pizza slices	1 packet Ranch dressing
1 package Chunk chicken	3 tablespoons Jalapeño cheese
¼ teaspoon Coriander seasoning	2 Jalapeño peppers (sliced)

Squeeze chicken pouch until the chunks of chcken feel shredded. Pour into bowl and stir in cheese, seasoning and crushed chips. Set aside. Carefully open one end of the pizze slice without tearing package. On a large chip bag, place the pizza slice. Cover with another chip bag. Use your insert cup as a rolling pin and flatten the slice until it's about ¼" thick. Place the slice back on pizza wrapper. Do the same for the other slice.

Divide the chicken mixture equally and place on ½ of each slice. Then, top the chicken with the sliced jalapeños and equal amounts of Ranch. Fold the other half of the slice over the chicken until the ends and side meet. Push the ends down with your thumbs.

Slide each pocket into a large brown bag or chip bag. The brown bag works the best. Clip the end almost closed, leaving enough room for the nozzle of the blow dryer. Tear a small hole in the other end so the air can get out. Heat for 1 hour, rotating after ½ hour.

Serves: 2

SUBSTITUTE: Try using 2 Spam singles or beef tips in place of the chicken. You can always use cream cheese in place of the jalapeño cheese no matter what type of meat is used.

DID YOU KNOW? Reindeer milk has more fat than cows milk.

Quick Nachos

1 package Chili with beans	1 Jalapeño pepper (diced)
¼ cup Jalapeño cheese	¼ bag Tortilla chips

Open chili pouch and add cheese, mix well. Heat in hot pot for at least 30 minutes. When hot, pour over chips and top with jalapeños. **Fast and filling!**

Serves: 1

VARIATION: Pour mixture over Salsa Verde or Nacho chips for a different flavor. And, chili with no beans is tasty too!

> **DID YOU KNOW?** A **True** vegetarian will eat nothing from an animal cooked or processed. A **Lacto** Vegetarian will eat dairy products. The only animal product that an **Ovo** vegetarian will eat is eggs. **Pesco** vegetarians will not eat red meat. They will eat fish, chicken, eggs, and dairy products.

Retha's Stuffed Spam Sandwiches

2 packages Spam singles	4 slices Bread
1 handful BBQ chips (crushed)	2 packets Cream cheese
1 teaspoon Jalapeño cheese	4 teaspoons Sandwich spread

Slice the Spam to make a "pocket". Set aside. In a large bowl, mix everything together. Stuff the Spam. Spread 1 teaspoonful of the sandwich spread on each slice of bread. Place Spam in between 2 slices of bread.

Place sandwiches separately inside chip bags and cook for 45 minutes. Remove from hot pot. Then heat with blow dryer in cereal bag or brown bag for 10 minutes to make "crispy".

Serve with your favorite chips or potato salad.

Serves: 2

> **DID YOU KNOW?** "Snickers" is named after 1 of the favorite horses of Frank Mars, who created the Snickers candy bar and founded Mars, Inc. The idea for the Snickers came from an already existing snack that was made up of nougat, peanuts, and caramel. Frank Mars added chocolate, put it in candy bar form, and started selling it wholesale. The Snickers bar quickly rose to being the world's most popular candy bar and has sustained that to this day. Annual sales of Snickers bar's total around $2 billion with about 1.5 million Snickers bars produced every day using about 100 tons of peanuts.

Sausage Fold Over

1 Summer Sausage	2 packets Ranch dressing
4 Flour tortillas	2 packets Cream cheese
1 Jalapeño pepper (diced)	Jalapeño cheese to taste
1 packet Beef soup seasoning	1 package Cheese-n-Chive crackers (crushed)
1 bag Jalapeño chips (crushed)	1 packet Chile soup seasoning

Slice Summer Sausage into about 20 pieces of meat and set aside. In a bowl, combine soup seasonings with jalapeño chips.

Squirt desired amount of cheese on the tortillas. With a spoon, spread the cheese to cover the entire tortilla. On half of tortillas place 5 pieces of meat. Evenly sprinkle chip mixture over meat. Add cream cheese, Ranch dressing, crushed crackers, jalapeño pepper and fold over.

Cook 2 hours in a chip bag. Serve with rice and beans.

Serves: 2

DID YOU KNOW? By feeding hens certain dyes they can be made to lay eggs with multi-colored yolks.

Something's Fishy in the Rice Paddy

3 packages Mackerel	4 tablespoons Jalapeño cheese
2 packets Soup seasonings (any flavor)	½ bag Pork skins (lightly crushed)
½ bag Rice	½ Pickle (chopped)
1 bag Peanuts (hot preferred)	1 Jalapeño pepper (chopped)
1 packet Ranch dressing	Water

Cook rice and soup seasonings together (adding water according to package directions) and set aside until cool. (This is a cold dish.) Place fish, Ranch dressing, peanuts, squeeze cheese, and jalapeños into another bowl. Add the pork skins and pickles and mix well (add a small amount of cold water if needed or pickle juice).

Divide equally into 3 bowls. Top with corn chips (if desired).

Serves: 3

SUBSTITUTE: Top with Salsa Verde or Nacho chips instead of the corn chips for a zesty flavor. Try cream cheese in place of the Ranch dressing for a milder taste. Tuna can replace the mackerel or 2 Spam singles can replace the Summer Sausage.

DID YOU KNOW? To make 1 kilo of honey, bees have to visit 4 million flowers, traveling a distance equal to 4 times around the earth.

Spicy Taco Pie

1 package Mexican beef	1 can Spicy V8 juice
1 packet Chili soup seasoning	1 Jalapeño pepper (chopped)
½ bottle Salsa	8 flour tortillas (cut up)
¼ bottle Jalapeño cheese	¼ bag Tortilla chips (crushed)

Set aside ¼ bottle cheese (heated), salsa, and crushed tortilla chips. Mix all other ingredients together and cook in a large cooking bag for two hours (make sure you double bag). When done pour into bowl. Top with tortilla chips, salsa, and cheese. **Olé**.

Serves: 2

DID YOU KNOW? Pine, spruce, or other evergreen wood should never be used in barbecues. These woods, when burning or smoking, can add harmful tar and resins to the food. Only hardwoods should be used for smoking and grilling, such as oak, pecan, maple, cherry, alder, apple, or mesquite. The choice depends on the type of meat being cooked.

Spicy Tuna Sandwiches

1 package Tuna	1 packet Chicken soup seasoning
½ packet Chili soup seasoning	1 tablespoon Pickle (diced)
1 Jalapeño pepper (diced)	½ cup Jalapeño chips (crushed)
6 tablespoons Salad dressing	Salsa (desired amount)
1 packet Ranch dressing	6 slices Bread

In a large bowl, mix everything together. Divide equally for 3 sandwiches. Serve with your favorite chips! Or, serve it with potato salad.

Serves: 3

SUBSTITUTE: Try using sandwich spread in place of the salad dressing. Chicken can be easily used in the place of the fish. Crushed Cheese-n-Chive crackers can be used as a substitute for the jalapeño chips for a milder sandwich. Just use more pickle instead of the jalapeños. **You will love it!**

DID YOU KNOW? On January 15, 1943, during World War II, bakers in the United States were ordered to stop using sliced bread for the duration of the war. Only whole bread was made available to the public. It was never explained how this action helped the war effort.

Stuffed Pickles

1 package Tuna	1 packet Chili soup seasoning
3 tablespoons Pickle juice	¼ teaspoon Mustard
1 packet Sweetener	½ jar Salad dressing
dash Hot sauce	¼ bag Salsa Verde chips (crushed)
4 Pickles (cut in half lengthwise and remove seeds)	¼ cup Jalapeño chips (crushed)
3 cups Cheese puffs (crushed)	1 bag Hot fries (crushed)

Combine the tuna, chili seasoning, pickle juice, mustard, sweetener, salad dressing, and hot sauce in a bowl and set aside for 30 minutes. Add the crushed chips to the mixture and mix well. Remove insides of pickle halves. Place 2 in each bowl.

Spoon the mixture into the 8 pickle halves. Then sprinkle the cheese puffs on top. Serve with your favorite crackers. **Delicious!**

Serves: 4

SUBSTITUTE: Mackerel can easily replace the tuna. For a sweet, yet spicy flavor use ½ BBQ chips in place of ½ of the jalapeño chips. You would be surprised at how good this will taste. And, if you are out of salad dressing, use a few packets of Ranch dressing and a couple cream cheese packets. You can always replace the salad dressing with sandwich spread, too.

> **DID YOU KNOW?** Egg yolks are one of the few foods that naturally contain Vitamin D.

Sweet & Sour Rice

1 Summer Sausage (diced)	1 Pickle (juice only)
1 bag Rice	1 packet Orange sports drink
2 bags Pork skins (crushed)	2 packets Ranch dressing
2 Lemon pies (filling only)	Water
1 teaspoon Instant coffee	

Cook rice in a large chip bag according to package directions, using all the pickle juice as part of the liquid needed and adding about ½ cup of water.

When done, add remaining ingredients and mix well. Cook for about 1 hour. Serve with your favorite crackers or chips. Eat pie crusts for dessert.

Serves: 2

SUBSTITUTE: Chicken or 2 Spam singles can be used in place of the Summer Sausage. Beef tips are also a delicious alternative using the gravy. Just decrease the amount of water and add the gravy to the pickle juice when cooking the rice.

> **DID YOU KNOW?** A coffee tree yields about one pound of coffee in a year.

Tabby's Creamy Chicken Alfredo

1 package Chunk chicken	½ teaspoon Black pepper
1 package Ramen Chicken soup	½ teaspoon Garlic salt
1 package Dry milk	1 teaspoon Onion flakes
1 packet Ranch dressing	Water
3 packets Cream cheese	

In an insert cup add everything except the noodles. Add just enough water to fill cup. Stir well. Cook for 45 minutes to 1 hour.

When chicken sauce is done, cook noodles according to package directions in another insert cup. Drain and divide evenly into two bowls. Pour sauce over noodles.

Serve with your favorite crackers.

Serves: 2

DID YOU KNOW? Chocolate contains phenylethylamine (PEA), a natural substance that is reputed to stimulate the same reaction in the body as falling in love.

Tamales

1 Summer Sausage	1 bag Corn chips (crushed)
1 packet Chili soup seasoning (for corn chips)	1 package Chili no beans
1 bag Salsa Verde chips (crushed)	1 bag Hot fries (crushed)
½ bag Jalapeño chips (crushed)	4 tablespoons Jalapeño cheese
1 Jalapeño pepper (diced)	Typing paper (cut in half sheets)
2 packets Beef soup seasoning (1 for meat & 1 for corn chips)	

In large bowl, combine corn chips, ½ Salsa Verde chips, Hot fries, 1 beef & chili seasonings. Stir well and set aside.

In another large bowl, mix meat (Summer Sausage & chili), beef seasoning, jalapeño chips, Salsa Verde chips, jalapeño pepper, and cheese until well blended. Continue to stir and add water to desired consistency.

Add a little water to corn chip mixture so it can easily be spread on paper. Top with meat mixture and roll up. Place in cooking bags. Cook about 2 hours.

Serves: 6

SUBSTITUTE: Use a package of Chunk chicken in place of the Summer Sausage and don't use the chili seasoning or one of the beef seasonings. Replace these with 1 chicken seasoning, 3 packets of Ranch dressing, and 3 packets of cream cheese.

DID YOU KNOW? Cheese is the oldest of all man-made foods.

II

Soups, Sides, Snacks & Dips

Bean dip

Jalapeños

Tortillia Chips

Alfredo Sauce

7 packets Cream cheese	1 packet Ranch dressing
¼ teaspoon Black pepper	

Mix everything together and serve over pasta or as a dip. It is wonderful over cooked chicken as well. **Very delicious!**

Serves: 2

DID YOU KNOW? No part of the banana is used to make banana oil. Banana oil, a synthetic compound is made with anyl alcohol and is named for its banana-like aroma.

Anytime Dip

¼ bottle Salsa	¾ jar Sandwich spread
1 packet Chili soup seasoning	

Put everything into a bowl and mix well. Return to the jar and replace lid. Serve over your favorite foods. It's also a delicious chip dip, too!

Serves: 10-12

DID YOU KNOW? The first American cookbook – called, appropriately, American Cookery – was published in 1796.

Chicken Flavored Rice

1 bag Rice	2 packets Chicken soup seasoning
1 Jalapeño pepper (diced)	¼ pickle (diced)

Prepare rice according to package directions. Add peppers, 1½ packets of the seasonings, and pickle into a large chip bag with the rice. Mix well. Cook 45 minutes to one hour.

VARIATION: For a meal, use a package of chunk chicken and add after rice is prepared. Or drain the gravy from beef-tips and use a beef soup seasoning for a hearty change.

Serves: 4

DID YOU KNOW? Carrots were once largely yellow, red, or purple. Today's orange color dates only from the 19th century.

Chili Soup

1 package Chili no beans	1 packet Chili soup seasoning
¼ bag 4-Cheese potatoes	¼ bag Jalapeño chips (crushed)
Jalapeño cheese (desired amount)	1 Jalapeño pepper (diced)
Water	2 tablespoons Pickle (diced)

Cook noodles according to package directions in a large chip bag. After draining off the water, add the remaining ingredients and mix well. You might need a little water to hydrate potatoes and chips. Cook at least 30 minutes.

Divide equally in 2 bowls and serve with your favorite chips or crackers.

Serves: 2

VARIATION: For an extra "spicy" soup, use a hot pickle and a teaspoon of habanero sauce. For a milder version, substitute BBQ chips for the jalapeño chips and increase the pickles and omit the jalapeño peppers.

DID YOU KNOW? Ice cream was originally made without sugar and eggs.

Cold Corn Chowder

¼ bag Cheese popcorn	¼ cup Jalapeño chips (finely crushed)
1 packet Chili soup seasoning	¼ Pickle (remove seeds and dice)
1 can V8 juice	2 Jalapeño peppers (diced)

In a large bowl, combine all ingredients except popcorn. Mix thoroughly. Transfer to a large chip bag and add the popcorn and shake until all the popcorn is coated. Pour into large bowl and serve with your favorite chips.

Serves: 3

DID YOU KNOW? Is bottled water worth it? 'Evian' spelled backwards is 'naïve'.

Creamy Cheese Dip

½ bottle Jalapeño cheese	1 Jalapeño pepper (diced)
1 packet Ranch dressing	3 packets Cream cheese
½ packet Chili soup seasoning	

In a large cooking bag, add all the ingredients and mix well. Heat for 45 minutes. Serve warm with your favorite chips.

Serves: 3

Crispy Tator Balls

1 bag Plain potato chips (crushed)	1 bag Hot fries (crush fine)
2 handfuls BBQ chips (crushed)	Black pepper to taste
2 handfuls Jalapeño chips (crushed)	Water
Salt to taste	

In a large bowl, pour in all of the chips except for the Hot fries. Crush the chips lightly to leave them "chunky". Add a little salt and pepper, if desired. Spoon water on the chips, a little at a time, and mix well. You just want them to hold together and not be mushy. Roll into about 10 balls.

Crush the Hot fries (in the bag) until they are a fine powder. Roll the balls in the Hot fries (in the bag) until they are well coated. Place these in a plastic cereal bag and lay it flat so the balls are not touching each other.

Heat with your blow dryer on low for about 20 minutes. Then, rotate the balls so you will be heating the other side. Heat on high for 10 minutes. You will think these came straight out of a convection oven. Serve with ketchup or your favorite dipping sauce.

Serves: 2

DID YOU KNOW? In South Africa, termites are often roasted and eaten by the handful, like pretzels or popcorn.

Delectable Cheese Fries

2 bags Nacho chips (crushed)	½ bottle Jalapeño cheese
Water	

Crush Nacho chips in bag and pour in a large bowl. Add a little water at a time until it is like the texture of dough.

Press out squares on a chip bag, one at a time. Squeeze the cheese down the middle of the square and roll up. Place on another chip bag so the fries are not touching.

When all of the fries are made, place inside a large brown bag or cereal bag and heat with blow dryer on high for about 40 minutes. Halfway through, rotate and turn for even cooking.

Serves: 2

SUGGESTION: Salsa Verde chips can be either combined with the Nacho chips for a different zesty flavor or used instead of the Nacho chips for variety.

DID YOU KNOW? In the winter, apple tree's need to "rest" for about 900-1,000 hours below 45 degrees Fahrenheit in order to flower and fruit properly.

Delicious Cheese Sauce

2 packets Cream cheese	4 tablespoons Jalapeño cheese
1 packet Ranch dressing	Black pepper (to taste)

Mix all ingredients together in an insert cup. Heat until creamy and stir until well combined. Can be used as dipping sauce. **This is delicious!**
Serves: 2

DID YOU KNOW? Watermelon is really a vegetable. It's cousin is the cucumber and its kin to the gourd. Watermelons can range in size from 7 pounds to 100 pounds.

Easy Crispy Tater Tots

1 bag BBQ chips (crushed)	2 tablespoons Jalapeño cheese
BBQ Sauce (desired amount)	

Crush chips in their bag. Pour into a large bowl. Add cheese and mix well. Form into tater tots and place in chip bag or cereal bag, in a single layer.
Cook with blow dryer for about 60 minutes. Turn them over after 30 minutes. Serve with BBQ sauce. **These are tasty!**
Serves: 2

DID YOU KNOW? Chocolate manufactures currently use 40 percent of the world's almonds and 20 percent of the world's peanuts in their confections.

Effortless Fish Chowder

1 package Mackerel	3 tablespoons Dry milk
1 Jalapeño pepper (chopped)	1 package Ramen Chili soup
2 packets Cream cheese	

Crunch up soup in package and then cook according to package directions. When done, drain off water and pour into a chip bag and add all ingredients together and mix well.
Cook in hot pot until everything is hot. It's so easy and so tasty! Serve with your favorite crackers.
Serves: 2

DID YOU KNOW? Apples are actually part of the rose family.

Fast & Hearty Soup

1 package Tuna	½ cup Rice
1 package Mackerel	1 can V8 juice (any flavor)
1 Summer Sausage (diced)	1 Jalapeño pepper (diced)

Pour everything into a large cooking bag and mix well. Double bag and cook in hot pot for at least 1 hour. Add a little water if necessary. Divide equally into 3 bowls and serve with your favorite crackers or chips.

Serves: 3

DID YOU KNOW? The citrus soda 7-Up was created in 1939. The "7" was selected because the original containers were 7 ounces, and "Up" indicated the direction of the bubbles.

Faux Pâté

1 package Chunk chicken	1 sleeve Snack crackers
2 Spam singles (diced)	3 tablespoons Salad dressing
10 packets Cream cheese	½ bag French Onion chips (crushed)
2 Jalapeño peppers (remove seeds and dice)	

In a large bowl, add chicken and Spam and mash together with spoon. Add chips and mix well, then set aside to allow chips to absorb moisture.

In another bowl, combine peppers and cheese and mix well. Add to meat mixture and mix well. Add the salad dressing and stir until creamy. Spread over crackers and enjoy them!

Serves: 4

SUBSTITUTE: For a different flavor, use sandwich spread in place of the salad dressing and use BBQ chips instead of the French Onion chips. Or, use jalapeño chips in place of the French Onion chips.

DID YOU KNOW? Mushrooms have no chlorophyll so they don't need sunshine to grow and thrive. Some of the earliest commercial mushroom farms were set up in caves in France during the reign of King Louis XIV (1638-1715).

Granola Bars

4 packages Maple & Brown Sugar oatmeal	1 package Multigrain/Caramel chips (crushed)
2 Vanilla Moon pies	3 Nutty bars (twin pack)
15 Butterscotch candies	2 packages Trail mix (crushed)

Open both Moon pies and remove the marshmallow filling. Place filling in your hot pot insert along with the 15 butterscotch candies. Add about 5 heaping spoonfuls of water to the insert. Place in hot pot and let cook until the butterscotch is completely melted with the marshmallow filling. This will take about 2 hours.

Crush both the Nutty bars and Multigrain/Carmel chips. Place in large bowl and combine with the 4 packages of oatmeal. Crush the Trail mix into small pieces and add to mixture in bowl and combine well.

Remove insert from hot pot and stir until both are well blended. Then pour over contents in bowl.

With clean hands, mash contents together. Spread on a chip bag and flatten out into a rectangle. Cut with spoon in 2 by 3 inch portions.

After cooling enjoy!

Serves: 4

SUBSTITUTE: Apple Cinnamon oatmeal can easily replace the Maple & Brown Sugar. If you want it less sweet, use one plain oatmeal packet in place of a flavored packet. If you want it more sweet, make a glaze from some cream filling from cookies and drizzle over the top.

> **DID YOU KNOW?** Capsaicin, which makes hot peppers, "hot" to the human mouth, is best neutralized by casein, the main protein found in milk.

Jalapinata's

1 package Chili no beans	1 package Mexican beef
1 cup Dried beans	8 packets Cream cheese
10 tablespoons Jalapeño cheese	2 cups Party mix (crushed)
2 cups Jalapeño chips (crushed)	24 Jalapeño peppers

Half each jalapeño pepper and clean out seeds and rinse in cold water. Place inside large bowl and set aside.

In another large bowl, combine all of the other ingredients and mix until well blended. Stuff each half of the jalapeños. Serve cold as an appetizer. **Enjoy!**

Serves: 8

> **DID YOU KNOW?** The first ring donuts were produced in 1847 by a 15 year old baker's apprentice, Hanson Gregory, who knocked the soggy center out of a fried *doughnut*.

Just a Dip

30 packets Cream cheese	3 teaspoons Pickle juice
¼ packet Beef soup seasoning	¼ packet Chili soup seasoning
¼ packet Chicken soup seasoning	

In a large bowl, squeeze out all of cream cheese from packets. Add pickle juice and seasonings. (Adjust seasonings to your preferred taste). Stir until everything is creamy.
Serve with your favorite crackers or chips.
Serves: 2

DID YOU KNOW? The first breakfast cereal was made by adding sugar and milk to popped popcorn. A shortage of baking flours after World War II forced bread makers to substitute up to 25 percent of wheat flour with ground popcorn. Over the years, popcorn also has been used as an ingredient to pudding, candy, soup, salads, and entrée's.

Layered Dip

¾ bag Jalapeño chips (crushed)	1 package Chili no beans
1 bag Corn chips (crushed)	½ bag Dried beans
3 Jalapeño peppers (diced)	½ bag Salsa Verde chips (crushed)
¼ bottle Salsa	¼ bottle Jalapeño cheese
10 packets Cream cheese	1 bag Tortilla chips

Prepare dried beans according to the package directions in a large chip bag. Mix jalapeño chips with 2 spoons of hot water and press into a large bowl. Set aside.
Mix chili with corn chips and pour into bowl with jalapeño chips. Add layer of beans and spread evenly.
Mix Salsa Verde chips with 2 spoons of hot water and spread over beans. Add cream cheese then salsa, jalapeño cheese and top with peppers. Enjoy with tortilla chips!
Serves: 6

VARIATION: Nacho chips can easily be substituted for tortilla chips. Or, use Nacho chips in place of the Salsa Verde chips and substitute the tortilla chips with Salsa Verde chips. You can always serve with Nacho, Salsa Verde and tortilla chips at the same time. **Have fun!**

DID YOU KNOW? An apple, onion, and potato all have the same taste. The differences in flavor are caused by their smell. To prove this – pinch your nose and take a bite from each. They will all taste sweet.

On Hand Cheese Sauce

1 bottle Jalapeño cheese	1 jar Sandwich spread
1 Hot pickle (diced)	2 Jalapeño peppers (diced)

Place the diced pickle and pepper pieces into a large bowl. Stir in the cheese and sandwich spread, mixing well.

Place back in their containers. This is a good sauce to have on hand. It tastes delicious and it can be used with anything.

Serves: 10-12

VARIATION: For a milder flavor use dill pickles instead of the hot pickles and use salad dressing instead of the sandwich spread. I like to remove the seeds from the pickle and peppers even though it doesn't alter the taste any.

DID YOU KNOW? Hush puppies are pieces of fried cornmeal batter which are a great southern tradition. Years ago, pieces of the fried batter were fed to hungry dogs that begged for food. After the scraps were given to the dogs, the owner would say "Now hush, puppy."

Penudo Soup

1 Summer Sausage (diced)	1 tablespoon Onion flakes
1 package Chili no beans	¼ bag rice
1 package Chili soup seasoning	4 Jalapeño peppers (diced)
1 cup Tortilla chips (broken up)	1 teaspoon Hot sauce
3 bags Pork skins (break up)	½ teaspoon Garlic powder
Water	

Cook rice according to package directions. When done, pour into a large chip bag.

Add remaining ingredients with about 1½ cups of water. Cook in hot pot for about 45 minutes. Add more water, if needed because it's a soup.

Serve with flour tortillas or crackers.

Serves: 2

SUBSTITUTE: 2 Spam singles are a good replacement for the Summer Sausage. And, Nacho chips and Salsa Verde chips can be used instead of the tortilla chips. Or, use equal amounts of all 3.

DID YOU KNOW? Most peaches that are imported to the United States during winter months come from Chili.

Pimienta Sauce

½ jar Salad dressing	½ jar Sandwich spread
1 packet Lemon Cool-down	1 packet Chili soup seasoning

Mix everything well in a large bowl. Use on sandwiches or as a dip for potato chips.
Serves: 10-12

☺ **HELPFUL HINT**: Leftover sauce can be stored in a jar for future use.

> **DID YOU KNOW?** Mayonnaise is said to be the invention of the French Chef of the Duke de Richelieu in 1756. While the Duke was defeating the British troops at Port Mahon, his Chef was creating a victory feast that included a sauce made of cream and eggs. When the Chef realized that there was no cream in the kitchen, he improvised, substituting olive oil for the cream. A new culinary masterpiece was born, and the Chef named it "Mayonnaise" in honor of the Duke's victory at Port Mahon.

Potato Soup

1 bag 4-Cheese potatoes	4 packets Cream cheese
1 bag Herb potatoes	1 package Cheese-n-Chive crackers (crumbled)
¼ bag Dry milk	Jalapeño cheese (to taste)
1 bag Pork skins (crushed)	Water

In large cooking bag, mix potato flakes and milk together. Add just enough hot water until it is the consistency of a thin chowder.

Cook in hot pot until steaming hot (about 1 hour). Pour into a bowl. Add squeeze cheese and cream cheese. Add more water as needed to thin out. Return to cooking bag. (Double bag). Cook 1 hour.

Pour evenly into 2 bowls and top with crushed pork skins and crackers.

Serve with your favorite crackers or chips.

Serves: 2

VARIATION: Summer Sausage chopped and added to soup mixture makes a hearty meal.

> **DID YOU KNOW?** Before Columbus, Europe had never tasted corn, potatoes, tomatoes, red peppers, sweet potatoes, tapioca, chocolate, pumpkin, squash, coconuts, pineapples, strawberries, and much more because these food items are native to America.

Quick Snack

1 bag Tortilla chips	4 tablespoons Jalapeño Cheese
1 bag Dried beans	1 package Shredded BBQ beef
1 package Chili no beans	1 Jalapeño pepper (sliced)

Cook beans separately according to package directions in a large chip bag. In another large chip bag, combine the cheese and sliced peppers together and heat.

Then, add the beans, chili, and beef and mix well. Cook all together for another 45 minutes. Serve with tortilla chips.

Serves: 2

SUBSTITUTE: Beef tips can be used in place of the BBQ beef. Cut each of the beef tips in half and drain off half of the gravy. Chicken can always be used, too. Just shred it by squeezing package together until you no longer feel the "cubes."

DID YOU KNOW? Goats milk is used more widely throughout the world than cows milk.

Salsa Caliente

½ bottle Habanero sauce	1 packet Chili soup seasoning
1 can V8 juice	¼ cup Pickle juice
8 Jalapeño peppers (diced)	1 Pickle (no skin, cut up small)

Place all of the ingredients in a peanut butter jar and fill with V8 juice. Shake well! This is not for sissies – **it's mucho caliente!**

Serves: Varied

DID YOU KNOW? Rice is the staple food of more than one half of the world's population.

Simple Relish

1 Pickle (diced)	1 teaspoon Pickle juice
4-5 Jalapeño peppers (diced)	1-2 packets Chili soup seasonings
2-3 packets Sweeteners	pinch Black pepper

Mix all together and store in a peanut butter jar. This is an excellent relish to have on hand.

Serves: 10-12

DID YOU KNOW? Coca-Cola was originally green.

Spicy Potato Salad

1 package 4-Cheese potatoes	¾ bag Jalapeño chips (crushed)
1 Jalapeño pepper (diced)	¼ Pickle (diced)
1 bag Hot fries (crushed)	1 packet Chili soup seasoning
Mustard (to taste)	Salad dressing (to taste)
Salt and pepper (to taste)	Water

Combine potatoes, chips, peppers, pickle, and seasoning in a large bowl and add hot water (a little at a time) while stirring. Continue mixing, making sure the chips are completely hydrated and there are no flakes remaining from the instant potatoes.

Add salad dressing and mustard to desired taste and consistency. Stir in a little salt and pepper to taste as well.

You will be surprised at this free-world taste! Serve as a side with your favorite sandwich.

Serves: 4

VARIATION: Use Herb potatoes in place of the 4 Cheese potatoes for a different flavor. If you want it a little "less spicy" use more pickles in place of the jalapeño's.

DID YOU KNOW? The most popular Campbell's Soup in Hong Kong is Watercress and Duck Gizzard.

Sweet & Sour Chicken Soup

1 package Chunk chicken	¼ cup Jalapeño cheese
1 package Ramen Chili soup	¼ cup Salad dressing
1 can Orange/Pineapple juice	Hot sauce (to taste)
1 package Trail mix	1 package Peanuts
1 Jalapeño pepper (remove seeds and dice)	

Cook soup according to package directions. When done, drain off water and place in a large chip bag. Add juice, trail mix, nuts, peppers, cheese, and salad dressing and mix well. Place in another chip bag and cook about 45 minutes.

When done, divide into 2 bowls and sprinkle with hot sauce, if desired. Serve with your favorite chips or crackers.

Serves: 2

VARIATION: You can use 2 Spam, tuna or Summer Sausage in place of the chicken. For a more tangy flavor, try using sandwich spread in place of the salad dressing. A spoonful of diced pickles taste good, too.

DID YOU KNOW? Honey is believed to be the only food that does not spoil.

Soups, Sides, Snacks & Dips

Sweet & Sour Relish

1 Jalapeño pepper (diced)	1 packet Peach Cool-down
1 Pickle (diced)	2 packets Sweeteners
1 packet Chili soup seasoning	1 can V8 juice

After dicing the pickle and peppers place in an empty peanut butter jar. Add seasoning, sweetener, V8 juice, and Cool-down. Replace top and shake until mixed well.

This is good over soup, chips, or rice. **WOW!**

Serves: 6-8

VARIATION: For more spice, use more jalapeño peppers and add hot sauce. For an even "hotter" relish, use a hot pickle instead of the dill.

DID YOU KNOW? A person swallows approximately 295 times while eating a meal.

Tangy Mayo Sauce

1 jar Salad dressing	½ packet Chili soup seasoning
2 teaspoons Mustard	dash Lemon Cool-down

Mix the first 3 ingredients together in a bowl. Add the Lemon Cool-down, a little at a time. Return to jar.

This is great for Spam sandwiches, chicken tacos, or tuna dishes.

Serves: 10-12

SUBSTITUTE: The salad dressing can always be replaced with sandwich spread. If you do this, then increase the mustard by another teaspoonful.

DID YOU KNOW? Pepsi-Cola was originally called "Brad's drink."

Tangy Mustard

1 jar Mustard	1 packet Chili soup seasoning
dash Lemon Cool-down	

Combine everything and mix well in the jar. This makes an excellent spread for sandwiches. It's also a good dip.

Serves: 10-12

DID YOU KNOW? The world's oldest piece of chewing gum is 9000 years old!

Tator Tots

1 package 4-Cheese potatoes	1 bag Hot fries (crushed)
1 bag Pork skins (crushed)	½ cup Jalapeño chips (crushed)
Water	3 tablespoons Jalapeño cheese
Typing paper (each sheet torn into 4 pieces)	

Into a large bowl, crush the hot fries and pork skins and mix together. Set aside (this will be the coating).

In another large bowl, mix potatoes with hot water, making them stiff. Roll into individual balls. Make a small hole in the center and fill with cheese. Close up and roll in chip mixture until coated well.

Place each one on typing paper and roll up and place in a large chip bag. Cook one hour. Dip in ketchup or your favorite sauce.

Serves: 4

VARIATION: For a milder flavor, use cream cheese in place of the jalapeño cheese. Herb potatoes can replace the 4 cheese potatoes. Or, place inside a cereal bag (without the typing paper) and heat with hair dryer for about 1 hour. Turn after 30 minutes. **These will be crispy!**

DID YOU KNOW? Refried beans are only fried once. The reason for this misconception is a translation error. The originals are frijoles refritos which actually means "well fried beans"—not re-fried.

The Old Stand-By Sauce

2 packets Ranch dressing	3 packets Cream cheese
2 tablespoons Jalapeño cheese	dash Season-All

Mix everything well and heat in an insert cup for 45 minutes. This makes a good sauce for burritos, when you want a change. Or, try it on any of your favorite foods.

Serves: 2

DID YOU KNOW? Coconut water can be used (in emergencies) as a substitute for blood plasma. The reason for this is that coconut water (the water found in coconuts – not to be confused with coconut milk, which comes from the flesh of the coconut) is sterile and has an ideal Ph level. Coconut water is liquid endosperm – it surrounds the embryo and provides nutrition.

Tortilla Soup

1 package Mexican meat	1 cup Tortilla chips
2 packages Ramen Beef soup	2 tablespoons Jalapeño cheese
1 cup Salsa Verde chips	1 teaspoon Hot sauce
2 packets Cream cheese	

Cook noodles according to package directions in large cooking bag. When done, drain off the water and add the meat to the soup. Cook 45 minutes. Add cheeses and hot sauce. When melted and mixed well, divide into 2 bowls.

Top both bowls with equal amounts of tortilla chips and Salsa Verde chips. Serve immediately.

Serves: 2

DID YOU KNOW? Mincemeat was originally a medieval food made of a sweet, spicy mixture of chopped lean meat, (usually beef, or beef tongue), suet and fruit. Over time, the meat content was reduced, and today the mixture contains nuts, dried fruit, beef suet, spices and brandy or rum, but usually no beef.

Tuna Noodle Soup

1 package Tuna	2 packets Cream cheese
2 packages Ramen Chicken soup	3 tablespoons Jalapeño cheese
1 cup Jalapeño chips (lightly crushed)	Cheese nips (broken up) (desired amount)

In a large chip bag, cook soups according to package directions. Then, add tuna, cheese (both) and cook until melted and blended for about 30 minutes.

Pour into 2 bowls and top with crackers and chips. Eat immediately.

Serves: 1

SUBSTITUTE: Mackerel can replace the Tuna without changing anything else. 1 Ranch dressing can be used in place of the 2 cream cheese or the jalapeño cheese. Or, drizzle a little Ranch dressing on top as an addition to the cheese.

DID YOU KNOW? Research has shown that allowing chocolate to melt in your mouth produced brain and heart rate activity that was similar to – and even stronger than – that produced with passionate kissing. WOW!

Ultimate Guacamole Dip

1 bag Salsa Verde chips (crushed)	2-3 tablespoons Salad dressing
½ bag Hot fries (crushed fine)	½ cup Salsa
1 Jalapeño pepper (diced)	½ packet Lemon-Cool-down
dash Chili soup seasoning	

In a bowl, add all the dry ingredients except the Cool-down. Mix well. Slowly stir in the salad dressing and salsa until you reach the desired consistency. Make sure everything is combined well.

Then, add the Cool-down, a little at a time, until you have the desired taste. Serve with tortilla chips. **Ole'!**

Serves: 4

DID YOU KNOW? Candy maker Milton S. Hershey switched from making caramels to chocolate in 1903 because caramels didn't retain the imprint of his name in summertime and the chocolate did.

Zesty Beans

1 package Dried beans	1 Jalapeño pepper (diced)
2 packets Cream cheese	2 tablespoons Jalapeño cheese
2 packets Ranch dressing	¼ cup Jalapeño chips (crushed)
1 packet Beef soup seasoning	¼ cup Salsa Verde chips (crushed)
1 Pickle (diced)	Salsa (desired amount)
Water	

In a large chip bag, mix all ingredients together until well blended. Add enough water to hydrate beans and chips then mix well. Cook 45 minutes.

Serves: 6 (as a side dish)

DID YOU KNOW? When Birdseye introduced the first frozen food in 1930, what did the company call it? "Frosted Food." Company officials feared the word frozen would suggest flesh burns. The name was changed to "frozen food" soon after.

Just Desserts

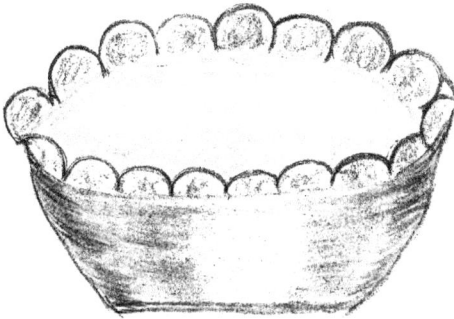

Banana Pudding

Parfait

Lava Cake

A Mudslide in the Pen

1 package Chocolate chip cookies	1 Chick-O-Stick (crushed)
1 Snickers candy bar	8 Malted chocolate balls (crushed)
1 bag Chocolate covered peanuts (½ melted)	1 Hershey's plain candy bar (melted in wrapper)
1 Moon pie (any flavor) (wet)	pinch Cappuccino (any flavor)

In a large bowl, crush cookies until fine and add water as needed, mixing well (slowly until it resembles a dough). When cookies are firm, form a ball and put ½ of the ball in another large bowl. Press into a crust on the bottom and up the sides of the bowl. Add ½ bag of chocolate covered peanuts and press into the crust.

Layer Chick-O-Stick, malted balls, wet Moon pie, and ½ of the Snickers on top. Press everything down.

In an insert cup, melt the remaining chocolate covered peanuts. When melted, add the cappuccino with a small amount of hot water. Stir until it is a thick glaze. Pour on top of everything.

Smash the other cookie ball into a patty (in your clean hands) and place over the entire cake. Press to seal it together. Crumble the rest of the Snickers over the top and lightly press into dough. Tear off end of the melted Hershey's bar and drizzle all over the top.

Serves: 6

VARIATION: If you want even more chocolate then increase your Snickers to 2 candy bars. And use 2 Hershey's plain candy bars. Or, add a Milky Way to your Snickers. You can never have too much chocolate.

☺ **HEALTHFUL HINT:** Always wash your hands with soap and water before you begin cooking.

DID YOU KNOW? Microwave cooking was discovered accidentally, when a chocolate bar melted in someone's pocket. This is very true and very scary – imagine what it was doing to his leg! The fact is, Percy LeBaran Spencer of the Raytheon Company was walking past a radar tube and he noticed that the chocolate bar in his pocket melted. He then tested popcorn in front of the tube (surely turning up the power and standing out of the beam), and it quickly popped all over the room. He is (obviously) known as the inventor of the Microwave oven.

Almond Joy Cake

1 package Macaroon cookies (crushed)	12 Almonds (crushed)
3 Almond Snickers (melted)	2 Milky Way candy bars (melted)
¼ cup Hot chocolate drink mix	3 tablespoons Dry milk
8 packets Sweeteners	Water
1 package Chocolate cream cookies (separate and crush)	

In a large bowl, combine crushed macaroon cookies with milk and sweeteners. Add about 6 spoonfuls of water and stir until mixed well. Transfer to a cooking bag and cook for 1 hour.

Remove filling from cookies and crush. In an insert cup, add filling to Milky Ways and melt in hot pot. Stir well. In a large bowl combine cookies with hot chocolate and add 6 spoonful's of water. Stir well and press into bowl.

Melt Almond Snickers in hot pot leaving them in the wrapper. Spread melted Almond Snickers over cookies. Let set 1 hour. Spread the hot cookies evenly and top this with melted Milky Way mixture. Sprinkle crushed almonds over this. It tastes even better while still warm.

Serves: 6

DID YOU KNOW? Strawberries have more Vitamin C than oranges.

Almost Banana Boast

1 package Macaroon cookies	4 Cherry pies
4 Banana Moon pies	1 pint Banana Pudding ice cream
Water	

Break apart the Moon pies and place in an insert cup and melt completely with a little water.

In a large bowl, crush cookies and make crust by adding a spoonful of water, at a time, to form cookies into dough. Do not make too wet. Mold into a pie crust in the large bowl.

In another bowl, combine the ice cream with melted Moon pies. Whip them into the ice cream. Pour this into the crust and spread evenly.

Let cake sit for about 30 minutes. Scrape cherry filling from pies (try to keep crust whole) and place on top of the cake. Spread evenly.

Place cherry pie crust over the filling and pack on top to make an even layer over the entire pie. Let set for at least 1 hour.

Serves: 6

VARIATION: Add Chunks of a Milky Way candy bar into the ice cream and Moon pie mixture. Then, drizzle a melted Hershey's candy bar over the Cherry pie crust.

DID YOU KNOW? West Africa produces nearly 70% of the world's cocoa.

Amazing Cheesecake

1 pint Coconut Fudge ice cream	2 bags Dry milk
1 package Chocolate cream cookies (separate & crush)	4 tablespoons Hot chocolate drink mix
1 package Macaroon cookies	8 packets Sweeteners
2 Hershey's with Almonds candy bars	2 Almond Snickers candy bars
1 package Trail mix (almonds only)	Water

Let ice cream melt in container. Remove cream from cookies and place both types of cookies into 2 large bowls. Put filling in an insert cup and set aside. Crush cookies in large bowls separately, and set macaroons aside. Add hot chocolate to chocolate cookies and combine. Add 3 spoons of water and mix well. Press into the bottom and sides of the bowl.

Add 6 spoons of warm water to 2 spoons of milk and mix well. Pour over macaroon cookies and mix well. Set aside.

Remove the almonds from the Hershey's bars and set them aside. Add the candy bars to the cooking filling and melt in hot pot. Melt Snickers bars separately in their wrappers in the hot pot along side the insert.

Pour melted ice cream into a large bowl. Add remaining dry milk and sweeteners. Mix well. It will be stiff. Spread 3 heaping tablespoons of this over the chocolate cookie shell. Crumble the macaroon cookie mix on top of this.

Add a small amount of water to filling (stirring gently). Spread over the crumbled macaroons. Press almonds (from the Hershey bars) down into mix randomly. Let set about an hour.

Then, spread chocolate filling mixture on top of this.

Remove almonds from the Trail mix and crush, and sprinkle them on top and let set about 3 more hours. **It is well worth the wait!**

Serves: 6

DID YOU KNOW? Blueberry juice boosts memory.

Banana Best Pie

¾ bag Vanilla wafers	4 Moon pies (Banana)
1 pint Banana Nut ice cream (melted)	

Let ice cream melt in container and crumble the Moon pies into a large bowl. Layer bottom of another large bowl with wafers.

When melted, combine ice cream with Moon pies and mix well. Spread a layer of ice cream mixture over wafers. Repeat the process 2 or 3 times until all ingredients are used up.

Crumble about 6 wafers to use as the last topping. Let set for about 2 hours. **Yum!**

Serves: 4

DID YOU KNOW? There are approximately 61,269 pizza restaurants in the United States.

Banana Fudge Pie

1 package Energizer nut mix	½ cup Chocolate syrup
2 Banana Fudge ice creams	Water
1 package Vanilla cream cookies (separated and crushed)	

Separate cream filling from cookies and melt filling in hot pot insert adding a little bit of water. Stir well. Let the ice cream melt in packages.

In a large bowl, crush the cookies. Add the chocolate, a little at a time, while stirring to make sure it is well blended. Don't let it get too wet. It needs to be doughy. Add the Energizer mix and work it in with your hands. Shape it to the bottom of the bowl for the crust.

In another bowl, combine the melted ice cream and the cookie filling. Whip it until it's smooth. Pour it into the crust and let set at least 2 hours.

Serves: 4

SUBSTITUTE: If you are a chocolate lover, try using Double Fudge cookies in place of the Vanilla cookies. You will be pleased!

DID YOU KNOW? Pretzels were originally invented for Christian lent.

Banana Nutty Cheesecake

1 pint Banana Nut ice cream	2 bags Dry milk
1 package Mixed nuts	2 Cupcakes (any flavor) (cream filling only)
2 Oatmeal pies	1 teaspoon Chocolate syrup
3 Banana Moon pies (separate marshmallow filling from cake)	

Separate the marshmallow filling from the Moon pies and set aside. Remove the cream filling from the cupcakes and set aside.

In a large bowl, combine the Banana Nut ice cream with the two packages of dry milk. Mix well. Set aside.

In a hot pot insert, hydrate the banana chips in hot water. When they become soft, drain off the water and add the marshmallow filling. Crush the nuts and add while mixing well. Continue to heat until the filling is melted and all is creamy. Stir frequently.

In another large bowl, smash all of the Oatmeal pies and add the Moon pie cake parts and mix well. Form this mixture into a crust on the bottom and up the sides of the bowl. Press firmly.

Pour the ice cream mixture over the crust. Top with the cream filling from the cupcakes. Then drizzle chocolate syrup over the top. Let cheesecake set for at least an hour.

Eat the cupcake parts while you are waiting for the cheesecake to set.

Serves: 6

SUBSTITUTE: 2 packages of Energizer nut mix can be used in place of the mixed nuts. A melted Hershey's candy bar can replace the chocolate syrup.

Banana O' Rama Cake

1 pint Moollenium Crunch ice cream (melted)	1 Hershey's plain candy bar
2 Nutzo ice cream bars (remove cones & crush in package)	5 Banana Moon pies
1 pint Banana Split ice cream (for bananas)	1 bag Vanilla wafers

Break up Moon pies into bite size pieces and place in a large bowl and set aside. In another large bowl, line the bowl with whole Vanilla wafers and be sure to go up the sides of the bowl.

In another large bowl, mix together the ice cream and just the ice cream from the 2 Nutzo's. Crumble Nutzo cones together with Moon pies. Fold into the ice cream mixture and mix well. Pour over the top of the crust. It will fit in the bowl. Just be careful.

In another large bowl, dump in the Banana Split ice cream and remove the banana's. Place the Banana's on top and drizzle with the melted Hershey. Let set about 2 hours.

Eat all the Banana Split ice cream.

Serves: 6

DID YOU KNOW? The same chemicals that give tart cherries their color may relieve pain better than aspirin and ibuprofen in humans.

Banana Pudding Treat

3 Banana Moon pies	1 bag Vanilla wafers
1 pint Banana Pudding ice cream (melted)	1 teaspoon Butter
1 package Energizer nut mix (crushed and remove fruit pieces)	

Break up the Moon pies and place inside an insert cup. Add the butter to this and melt together until it's the consistency of pudding. Stir frequently. Combine this with melted ice cream in a large bowl and mix well.

In another large bowl, arrange a layer of Vanilla wafers so sides touch and they do not overlap. Cover with 1/3 of the banana mixture. Then add another layer of wafers and repeat until the mixture is gone.

Top with the Energizer mix (with the banana and other fruit pieces removed). Let set for at least 1 hour before serving. Eat all the fruit pieces while you are waiting for it to set.

Serves: 6

VARIATION: Banana Nut ice cream makes a good banana pudding dish, too. You can always melt a Hershey's plain candy bar and swirl on top. Strawberry preserves also make an unusual and tasty topping for that special occasion.

DID YOU KNOW? The canning process for Herring was developed in Sardinia, which is why canned Herrings are better known as Sardines.

Banana Sensation

1 Banana Split ice cream (melted)	1 bag Vanilla wafers
5 Banana Moon pies	

Let ice cream melt in container. In a large bowl, break up the Moon pies and form a crust in bowl on bottom and up the sides. Pour 1/3 of the melted ice cream over crust and spread evenly.

Top this with a layer of Vanilla wafers (sides touching). Repeat 2 more times until all ice cream is used and the last layer is the Vanilla wafers.

Cover and let set for at least 3 hours.

Serves: 4

SUBSTITUTE: Banana Nut ice cream can replace the Banana Split if they are out at the commissary. For a completely different flavor, try using Butter Crunch ice cream.

It's a nice treat!

DID YOU KNOW? 25% of all retail establishments in the U.S are for eating or drinking.

Banana Split Party Cheesecake

1 Hershey's plain candy bar (melted in wrapper)	12 Sweeteners
2 Cherry pies (remove filling)	1 Lemon pie
1 bag Dry milk	1 pint Banana Split ice cream
4 packets Cream cheese	1 package Peanuts (crushed)
2 packages Buds Best Candy Chip cookies (crushed)	

In a large bowl, crush cookies. Then, mix cookies with a little water and form into crust on the bottom and up the sides of the bowl.

After removing the filling, place fillings in separate bowls. Crumble ½ lemon and ½ cherry pie over cookie crust and press it down.

In another bowl, add milk, 2 cream cheese and sweeteners with the melted ice cream (may add a little water) and stir to desired consistency. Add the rest of pie crust pieces and pour into crust. Let set about 3 hours.

Mix lemon filling with remaining cream cheese. Spread cherry filling over pie, then swirl lemon filling over it. Drizzle melted chocolate bar over top and add crushed peanuts. Let set about 3 or 4 more hours. Enjoy!

Serves: 6

SUBSTITUTE: 1 package of Trail mix or 4 teaspoons of Sunflower seeds can replace the peanuts.

DID YOU KNOW? In Japan, Gerber's top selling baby food is a sardine dish!

Basic Chocolate Pie

1 M&Ms plain (crushed)	3 bags Dry milk
3 tablespoons Peanut butter	½ cup Chocolate syrup
3 sleeves Graham crackers (crushed fine)	¼ cup Water

In a large bowl, combine graham crackers with a small amount of water to form a crust (damp but not wet). Press crust into the bottom and up the sides of the bowl.

In another large bowl, combine water, chocolate syrup, and peanut butter together. Mix until well blended. Add milk and continue stirring until its thick like pancake batter. Pour into crust.

Let set about 4 or 5 hours. Sprinkle with M&Ms on top.

Serves: 4

SUBSTITUTE: You can make your own chocolate syrup using hot chocolate mix and water. The lumps will disappear when you are stirring in the dry milk. (It's easier if you use hot water).

DID YOU KNOW? Dandelion root can be roasted and ground as a coffee substitute.

Berry Banana Cheesecake

1 pint Strawberry ice cream (melted)	1 package Strawberry cream cookies (separate & crush)
4 packets Cream cheese	1 can Strawberry soda
5 Banana Moon pies	1 Hershey's plain candy bar
2 sleeves Graham crackers (crushed)	2 Snicker's candy bar

Let ice cream melt in container. When melted, remove strawberries and set aside. Melt Snickers (in wrapper's) in hot pot.

Separate cream from cookies and place in insert. Heat until you can mix together to make it creamy.

In another large bowl, crush cookies. Add crumbled graham crackers and mix well. Add soda, a little at a time, until mixture forms into dough. Press into bottom and up the sides of a bowl to form a crust.

In another bowl, combine ice cream, cream cheese, and cream filling. Stir until well blended. When candy bars are soft, cut one end off and add. Stir well. Add dry milk a little at a time, while continually stirring, until it is thick and creamy. If you need a little more liquid, add a little of the soda. Pour into crust. Place strawberries from ice cream on top.

Melt Hershey's candy bar (in wrapper) in hot pot. Cut off one corner and drizzle over top of cheesecake. Let set at least 4 hours. Drink the remaining soda.

Serves: 6

DID YOU KNOW? Peanuts are not nuts. They are legumes.

Butterfinger Cheesecake

1 pint Butter Crunch ice cream	1 package Buds Best Butterfinger cookies (crushed)
2 bags Dry milk	1 can Sprite
1 Butterfinger candy bar	¼ cup Hot chocolate drink mix

In a large bowl, melt ice cream. Set aside. In another bowl, crush cookies and add enough Sprite to dampen. Add the Sprite a little at a time. Form into a crust on the bottom and up the sides of the bowl.

Slowly add milk to melted ice cream and whip with a spoon. When it starts to thicken, add a little Sprite and continue whipping until it become's thick and creamy and not too runny!

Break up candy bar and sprinkle over top. Pour mixture into crust and let set at least 3 hours.

Then in a cup, place hot chocolate mix and add 1-2 spoons of Sprite to make a thick fudge. Stir until it is not grainy or lumpy. Drizzle over top of cheesecake when it is set. **Delicious!**

Serves: 6

> **DID YOU KNOW?** Pumpkin rule of thumb: The darker the shell, the longer the pumpkin lasts.

Butterfinger Cheesecake 2

1 pint Butter Crunch ice cream (melted)	2 package Buds Best Butterfinger cookies (crushed)
3 bags Dry milk	1 can Sprite
1 Butterfinger candy bar (crumbled)	1 Hershey's plain chocolate bar (melted)

In a large bowl, crush and dampen cookies with the Sprite to form into a curst. Add the Sprite, a little at a time, and set aside.

Mix ice cream with milk and add a little Sprite to a creamy consistency. Do not let it get too runny. Pour into crust. Let set about 2 hours.

Crumble Butterfinger over pie. Place Hershey's in hot pot to melt (leave in wrapper). When melted, cut end of wrapper off and drizzle over Butterfinger. Let set several hours.

Serves: 6

> **DID YOU KNOW?** Popcorn pops because water is stored in a small circle of soft starch in each kernel. As the kernel is heated, the water heats, the droplet of moisture turns to steam, and the steam builds up pressure until the kernel finally explodes to many times its original volume.

Butterfinger Lickin' Good Fudge

¼ cup Hot chocolate drink mix	2 tablespoons Dry milk
½ bag Vanilla wafers	1 package Vanilla cappuccino
1 package Oatmeal (plain)	5 Macaroon cookies (crushed)
3 tablespoons Chocolate syrup	1 Butterfinger candy bar (crushed)

Crush the Vanilla wafers in a large bowl. Add the hot chocolate and oatmeal and combine well. Add a little water at a time, and press to form a crust. Do not get too wet.

In another bowl, crush the macaroon cookies. Add the milk and cappuccino, chocolate syrup and 1 tablespoon of warm water. Mix well.

Pour this over the crust. Sprinkle the Butterfinger over the fudge. Let set 3 hours. You will not want to share this (with anyone)!

Serves: 2

VARIATION: 3 Chick-O-Sticks can easily replace the Butterfinger candy bar. For more chocolate flavor, break up a Milky Way candy bar and add after the chocolate syrup. Then drizzle a melted Hershey's over the Butterfinger.

DID YOU KNOW? Even though explorers had brought potatoes back from the New World in the early 1500s, Europeans were afraid to eat them for fear that the spuds would give them leprosy. It wasn't until Louis XVI, who was looking for a cheap food source for his starving subjects, served them at the royal table that people were convinced potatoes were safe to eat.

Butterscotch Brownies

1 package Vanilla wafers (crushed)	3 cups Hot chocolate drink mix
1 package Butterscotch candies (crushed)	Hot water

In a large bowl, combine crushed cookies with ½ of the crushed candies. Add all but ½ cup of hot chocolate and mix well.

Add hot water, a spoonful at a time, until the mixture resembles dough. Press the dough into the bottom and sides of the bowl.

In another bowl, combine the ½ cup hot chocolate and the other half of crushed candies. Add a little hot water and stir until it is a semi-thick glaze. Pour the glaze over the brownie.

Let set for at least an hour.

Serves: 4

DID YOU KNOW? Table salt is the only commodity that hasn't risen dramatically in price in the last 150 years.

Butterscotch Surprise

1 package Duplex cream cookies	1 bag Vanilla wafers
1 bag Butterscotch candies	½ can Sprite
½ jar Peanut butter	½ bag Dry milk

In an insert cup, melt butterscotch candies and mix with Sprite (you will probably use only ½ can). You want it to be thick and creamy. Let cool.

Remove filling from duplex cookies and add to peanut butter. Heat for about 30 minutes in hot pot insert so it is easier to combine them.

In a large bowl, crush cookies and Vanilla wafers and mix together. Add enough butterscotch mixture to moisten. Press into bowl. Combine milk with peanut butter mixture and the remaining butterscotch mixture, stirring until creamy. Pour this over cookies and spread evenly. Let set, then enjoy.

Serves: 6

DID YOU KNOW? Three quarters of fish that are caught are eaten. The rest are used to make things such as glue, soap, margarine, and fertilizer.

Candylicious Oatmeal Cookies

3 packages Plain oatmeal	1 3-Musketeers candy bar
3 packages Maple & Brown Sugar oatmeal	1 M&Ms plain candies
3 tablespoons Peanut butter	Water

Melt the peanut butter and 3-Musketeers in a hot pot insert. In a large bowl, add the oatmeal and a little water and stir in peanut butter mixture. Don't get it too wet. Mix well and add the M&Ms.

Take a large spoonful and form into ball and then smash down on a chip bag to form a cookie. Let cookie set to firm up. Then enjoy!

Serves: 4 (12-14 cookies)

SUBSTITUTE: Try a Milky Way in place of the 3-Musketeers for a caramel taste. And, M&Ms peanut candies can always be used in place of the plain ones, if you like it crunchier with a nutty flavor.

DID YOU KNOW? The table fork was introduced into England in 1601. Until then, people would eat with their knifes, spoons or fingers. When Queen Elizabeth first used a fork, the clergy went ballistic. They felt it was an insult to God to not touch meat with one's fingers.

Celeste's Signature Choc-O-Lotta Cake

5 Milky Way candy bars	2 Hershey's plain candy bars
6 packets Cream cheese	3 tablespoons Dry milk
½ bag Hot chocolate drink mix	Water
1 package Double Fudge cookies (separate and crush)	

Separate filling from cookies and place the cookies in a large bowl and the filling in an insert cup.

Frosting: Break apart the Hershey's and add to filling. In another cup, make a thick mixture of "syrup" using the hot chocolate, 1 tablespoon of the milk, and water. Add the water a spoonful at a time because you want it thick, like "syrup" and not too runny. Add about 5 tablespoons of this syrup to the cream filling mixture with 2 packets of cream cheese and mix all together. Cook in hot pot, stirring occasionally, until all is well blended and melted together. Don't overcook.

Cake: In the large bowl, crush cookies into pea size pieces. Add the 4 remaining cream cheese packets to the rest of the "syrup" and 2 tablespoons of milk and stir well. If it is too thick, you can thin with no more than 1 or 2 teaspoons of hot water. Add the syrup mixture to your cookies, a little at a time, and mix well. Leave it a little lumpy because the moisture will soften cookies as it sets and it won't be mushy.

Place ½ of the mixture into another large bowl and pack down. Open the Milky Ways and flatten them in your "clean hands" until they have tripled in width. Arrange each on top of cookie mixture so they cover it entirely with sides touching. Place the other half of the cookie mixture on top of this and make sure to cover the Milky Ways evenly. Press down.

The frosting mixture should be completely melted and mixed thoroughly. Pour over the top of the cake and spread out with your spoon. Set aside. It needs at least 2 hours to set. **Everyone loves this cake!**

Serves: 6

DID YOU KNOW? Banana's have no fat, cholesterol or sodium.

Cinnamon Roll Sandwich

2 Cinnamon rolls	4 tablespoons Strawberry preserves
2 packets Cream cheese	

Remove cinnamon rolls from package. Spread the cream cheese on top of one. Then spread the strawberry jam evenly over the cream cheese. Place 2nd cinnamon roll on top. Cut in half and place each half in a dry milk bag. Heat for 30 minutes. Share with a friend while enjoying your morning coffee.

Serves: 2

VARIATION: A cherry cinnamon roll really tastes delicious with the strawberry jam! And, so does a Honey Bun, believe it or not.

Chocolaska

3 Hershey's with almonds	1 pint Chocolate ice cream (melted)
2 bags Dry milk	4 packets Cream cheese
1 package Macaroon cookies (crushed)	Water

Let ice cream melt in container. In a large bowl, crush cookies, leaving a little chunky. You don't want them finely crushed. Add water, a spoonful at a time. Mix well. You want the cookies just moist enough to stick together and form a crust in the bottom and sides of the bowl.

In another large bowl, pour in the melted ice cream. Remove almonds from Hershey's and crush the almonds. Add to ice cream. As you remove almonds from 2 of the candy bars, break candy bars into small pieces and add to the ice cream. Put the chocolate pieces from the 3rd candy bar into an insert cup. Also, add 2 of the cream cheese packets.

Add the milk, a little at a time while continuously stirring. You do not want any lumps. Use all of the milk. You can add a little water, if needed for a creamy consistency. Don't let it get thin. Pour into crust and let set 2-3 hours.

Melt the Hershey's bar with the last 2 cream cheese. Mix thoroughly, and then drizzle over top of pie.

Serves: 6

DID YOU KNOW? Yams and sweet potatoes are <u>not</u> the same thing.

Chocolate Delight

3 Chocolate Moon pies	½ bag Vanilla wafers
2 teaspoons Butter	1 bag Peanuts (crushed)
1 Milky Way candy bar	

Crumble the Moon pies into a large chip bag. Add the Milky Way and butter. Melt in hot pot until it is the consistency of pudding. Stir well.

In a large bowl, arrange 1 layer of Vanilla wafers on the bottom and 1 layer around the sides. Pour 1/3 of the mixture over them. Then, add another layer of Vanilla wafers and repeat process until the pudding mixture is gone. Add peanuts to top it off.

Let set for at least 1 hour.

Serves: 3

SUBSTITUTE: You can use 3 crushed Chick-O-Sticks or 1 crushed Butterfinger candy bar in place of the peanuts, if desired. It will make it extra sweet.

DID YOU KNOW? Scientists at Cornell University have identified 2 cancer fighting substances in the tomato: P-courmaric and Chorogenic acids.

Chocolatinas

1 bag Dry milk	15 pieces Butterscotch candies
1 package Chocolate chip cookies	1 Chick-O-Stick (crushed)
¾ cup Hot chocolate drink mix	2 packets Sweeteners
1 package Double Fudge cookies (separate and crush)	

Separate cream from cookies and place cream in an insert cup. Place the cookies in a large bowl.

Filling: Crush fudge cookies. Add the hot chocolate and mix well. Add a little water at a time, until it's a thick and a creamy consistency. Don't make it too thin.

Spread on 16 chocolate chip cookies, and top with another cookie. Set aside on a large chip bag.

Icing: Crush butterscotch candies and put in insert. Cover with about ¼ teaspoon of water. Heat until dissolved. Add to the filling in insert cup and mix well. Heat until creamy. Pour into bowl and combine with the milk and sweetener. Add more milk if you need it thicker.

Ice the tops of the sandwiches and then sprinkle the Chick-O-Stick on top.

Serves: 16 Cookie Sandwiches

DID YOU KNOW? The average child will eat about 1,500 peanut butter and jelly sandwiches by the time they graduate from high school.

Chocolaty Mousse Pie

4 Snickers candy bars	½ cup Hot chocolate drink mix
1 package Peanuts (crushed)	Water
1 All Holiday's Basic Cookie/Cake recipe	

Heat the candy bars in their wrappers in hot pot until soft. Spread the cookie mixture into a rectangular shape that is about ½ inch thick on a large chip bag.

Cut the end off the wrapper and spread the warm candy bars evenly over the cake. Top this with the crushed nuts. Roll into a large log and place in a large chip bag. Heat for 1 hour.

Make a quick glaze with the chocolate drink mix and a little hot water. Keep adding water a spoonful at a time until it is the consistency of a glaze. Divide into bowls and pour glaze over tap. This is best if served warm.

Serves: 6

SUBSTITUTE: Milky Ways, 3-Musketeers, or Almond Snickers will taste good, too. Or, try using one of each flavor for variety.

DID YOU KNOW? A pound of potato chips cost 200 times more than a pound of potatoes.

Chocoholics Pie

1 box Graham crackers	¼ cup Water
3 bags Dry milk	2 tablespoons Peanut butter
½ cup Chocolate syrup	Butter (as desired)

In a large bowl combine syrup, water, and peanut butter. Mix well and set aside.

Crush graham crackers and add water or butter (a spoonful at a time) until it is the consistency of dough. Form into a crust on the bottom and sides of large bowl. Be sure to leave about one inch from the top of the bowl.

Pour dry milk into another bowl and add the syrup mixture folding it in until it is thick and resembles the consistency of pancake batter. Pour this over crust. (You may have some of the mixture left over. If you do, just keep licking the bowl.)

Serves: 6

SUBSTITUTE: If you only have hot chocolate drink mix, add a little hot water to make chocolate syrup. Just stir until it's not lumpy or grainy. You won't be able to taste the difference.

☺ **TOPPING IDEAS**: Crushed Chick-O-Sticks, M&Ms, peanuts or trail mix all make excellent toppings, too.

DID YOU KNOW? It takes 40 gallons of maple tree sap to make one gallon of maple syrup.

Coffee Balls

1 package Double Fudge cookies (separate filling and crush)	1 tablespoon Instant coffee
4 tablespoons Hot chocolate drink mix	Water

Separate filling from cookies and place filling in insert cup and heat in hot pot until melted. Place cookies in a large bowl. Crush cookies into pea-sized pieces. Crush coffee into fine powder and add to cookies. Add ½ of the hot chocolate mix and mix well. Add a spoonful of water, a little at a time, until mixture resembles dough. Don't get too wet. Set aside. Put remaining hot chocolate into a bowl and set aside.

Pinch off the dough and roll into 1 inch sized balls. Then, cover balls with filling and roll in hot chocolate. Set on flattened chip bag to dry.

Serves: 4

VARIATION: For a stronger flavor, add another teaspoonful of coffee.

☺ **HELPFUL HINT:** Store balls inside the hot chocolate bag (with the drink mix) to keep them from sticking together.

DID YOU KNOW? 88% of milk is water and 12% is a solid substance that has food value.

Cupcake Delight

1 package Chocolate cupcakes (twin pack)	2 Hershey's plain candy bars

Slice cupcake horizontally and remove cream filling. Eat the filling.

Heat candy bars in their wrappers in hot pot. When melted cut off one end. Squeeze into hole in cupcake and replace top. Repeat for other cupcake.

Place in chip bag and heat in hot pot for 10-15 minutes. Serve warm.

Serves: 1

VARIATION: Melt 1 teaspoon of peanut butter with 1 Hershey's plain candy bar to fill in hole. And, the Vanilla cupcakes can easily replace the chocolate.

DID YOU KNOW? Bananas are most likely the first fruit ever to be grown on a farm.

Cupcake Extravagance

1 package Vanilla cupcakes (twin pack)	1 bag Plain potato chips (crushed and 2 whole)

Open cupcakes and remove filling and icing. Place cake parts in a bowl. Heat filling and icing in a hot pot and mix well. Don't overheat. Just heat long enough to combine.

Kneed cupcakes together until it is a doughy ball. Divide equally into 4 balls. In a bowl, flatten out into a thin square.

Crush all the potato chips except for 2. Cover cake layer with a fine layer of icing/filling mixture. Sprinkle on a fine layer of crushed chips. Repeat with next layer. Top it off with 1 whole chip.

Make another layered cake with remaining ingredients. Serve immediately.

Serves: 2

DID YOU KNOW? Pilgrims ate popcorn at the first Thanksgiving dinner.

DeEllen's Tummy Ticklers

2 packages Butter Cupcakes	4 Strawberry ice cream bars
2 packets Cream cheese	

Let ice cream bars melt in 2 insert cups. Remove icing from cupcakes and eat the icing now. When strawberry bars are melted, add the cream cheese and mix well. Pour equally over each of the 4 cupcakes. Enjoy!

Serves: 2

DID YOU KNOW? Spam stands for **S**houlder, **P**ork and H**am**.

DeEllen's Two Milk's Cheesecake

1 pint Ice cream (any flavor) (melted)	1 package Cream cookies (any flavor) (separate & crush)
2 bags Dry milk	Water

Crust: Separate cream from cookies and place cookies in a large bowl and crush. Add a little water to form a crust on bottom and sides of bowl. Save the filling (in cookie wrapper) for another recipe.

Filling: In another large bowl, place melted ice cream and both packages of milk. Add 2 spoonfuls of water and stir until combined. That's it! Just pour into crust and let set for a few hours. You will be surprised at how good this tastes!

Serves: 6

SUGGESTION: Strawberry Vanilla, Cherry/Vanilla, and Moollennium ice creams work the best. If you use any ice cream with cookies or cake inside (e.g., Banana Pudding) you will need to use a little more water so your cheesecake won't be dry.

DID YOU KNOW? A baked potato (with the skin) is a good source of dietary fiber (4 grams).

Dirty Mudslide

1 package Chocolate cream cookies (crushed)	1 Butterfinger candy bar (crushed)
2 Moon pies (separate marshmallows from patties)	1 Nutty bar (twin pack)
2 Milky Way candy bars (diced)	Water
2 tablespoons Peanut butter (melted)	

Separate the chocolate cookie from the cream filling. Save the cream filling (in the cookie wrapper) for another recipe. In a large bowl, crush the chocolate cookie as if you are making a cookie cake. Out of the crushed cookies, prepare six chocolate patties small enough to fit into 2 insert cups. You will have to form the patties using a little water.

In this order layer the ingredients into your cup: chocolate cookie patty, ½ marshmallow from Moon pie, ½ diced Milky Way bar, ½ Nutty Bars, and one tablespoon peanut butter.

Repeat the steps for the second layer. Top off with final layer being a chocolate patty and crushed Butterfinger.

Cook in hot pot for one hour. Enjoy!

Serves: 2

DID YOU KNOW? Microwave popcorn is the same as other popcorn except the kernels are usually larger and the packaging is designed for maximum popping ability.

Downhome Cheesecake

½ bottle Strawberry preserves	1 Hershey's plain candy bar (melted in wrapper)
40 packets Cream cheese	3 tablespoons Water
1 package Cream cookies (any flavor) (separate filling & crush)	

Separate cream filling from cookies and place each in separate bowls and crush the cookies. In the bowl with the cream filling, add the cream cheese and mix well until soft and creamy.

In the bowl with the crushed cookies, add water (one spoonful at a time) until the crumbs are moist and will pack into a crust. Do not let it get too wet. Form the crust to the sides and bottom of the bowl.

Pour in the filling and top with the strawberry preserves. Place candy bar (still in wrapper) in a hot pot to melt. When ready to use, just tear off one corner and squeeze. Swirl on top. Let set for about 2 hours until firm.

Serves: 6

VARIATION: Mix a couple packages of cream cheese with the strawberry preserves before topping the filling. Or, add chocolate syrup to crushed cookies instead of water for a rich chocolate flavored crust. Or, do both!

DID YOU KNOW? Cranberries are sorted for ripeness by bouncing them; a fully ripened cranberry can be dribbled like a basketball.

Easiest No Bake Cookies

4 packages Maple Brown Sugar oatmeal	4 packages Oatmeal (plain)
1 package Chocolate cream cookies (separate filing & crush)	½ jar Peanut butter

In an insert cup, combine the peanut butter and cream filling and heat until melted, stirring occasionally to mix well. In a large bowl, crush the cookies (you can leave a little lumpy).

Pour the peanut butter mixture into the cookie crumbs. Add the flavored oatmeal. Then, pour the plain oatmeal into the insert cup to remove all the peanut butter that is stuck to the sides. Then pour into mixture.

Kneed everything with clean hands until it resembles a firm (but soft) dough. Then roll into 1½ inch balls.

Makes about 30 cookies.

Serves: 6

VARIATION: Roll balls in crushed up Chick-O-Sticks or hot chocolate drink mix for a different taste. If you want a slight coffee taste, roll the ball into a cappuccino.

DID YOU KNOW? Pepper is the top selling spice in the world. Mustard is the second.

Easy Banana Pudding

1 bag Vanilla wafers (some crushed)	1 bag Dry milk
1 pint Banana Pudding ice cream (melted)	

In a large bowl, pour in the melted ice cream. While stirring continuously, add the dry milk a little at a time, so that it doesn't get lumpy. Whip it until it is thick and creamy.

Then, mix in about 1 cup of crushed Vanilla wafers. Line the bottom and sides of another bowl with whole Vanilla wafers. Pour in just enough filling to cover layer.

Then, add more wafers and alternate with filling until everything is used. Set aside for 4 hours. Share with your bunkies.

Serves: 6

DID YOU KNOW? Dried chili pepper wreaths are called "ritras"-a symbol of plenty and hope.

Exceptional Brownies

2 tablespoons Peanut butter	¼ bag Hot chocolate drink mix
2 sleeves Graham crackers	

Fill empty peanut butter jar, or hot pot insert, to the top with the hot chocolate. Add a little hot water and stir (or shake) until chocolate dissolves and is very gooey. Don't let it get runny.

Add two large spoonful's of peanut butter into the chocolate. Place the jar filled with chocolate and peanut butter into the hot pot and mix. Heat approximately 20 to 30 minutes to melt all together. (Stir frequently.)

In a large bowl, crush Graham crackers until very fine. When the chocolate and peanut butter have melted, pour it over the graham crackers in the bowl.

Mix well and add a little water if needed. You want it thick so that it will get firm. Press into your bowl. Let set for a couple of hours. **Enjoy!**

Serves: 4-6

SUBSTITUTE: Half (½) a bag of Vanilla wafers can be used in place of the Graham crackers. For even more chocolate taste, crush a Butterfinger candy bar with the peanut butter. I like to drizzle the top of everything with a melted Hershey! And, if you like nuts, add a few spoonfuls of peanuts to your brownies before pressing into the bowl.

DID YOU KNOW? Beer is made by fermentation caused by bacteria feeding on yeast cells and then defecating.

Honey Bun Cake

1 Milky Way candy bar	1 Honey Bun
1 package Cream cookies (any flavor) (separate & crush)	Water

Open cookie package carefully so you can tear ends and open completely to use as a rectangle.

Separate cream from cookies and place in bowl. In another large bowl crush cookies. Add a spoonful of water, a little at a time, to mix with cookies until it forms into a dough.

Flatten dough on a cookie wrapper leaving about 2 inches from edge of wrapper on three sides and using only about ½ of the wrapper (lengthwise).

Place Honey Bun on top of dough so that edge of Honey Bun (lengthwise) is close to the end of the dough on the same side as the 2 inch front edge.

On the other end of the wrapper (that is empty) flatten Milky Ways with insert cup. Place this on top of Honey Bun. Sprinkle about ½ of the cream filling on top of candy bar.

Roll cake together starting at the front edge. Then place in chip bag (removing the cookie wrapper) and cook for at least 1 hour.

Melt the rest of cream filling in an insert cup and pour over cake before serving. (You may need to add a little water). **Enjoy!**

Serves: 6

DID YOU KNOW? Girls have more taste buds than boys.

Lemon Cheesecake

5 packets Cream cheese	3 packets Lemon Cool-downs
2 bags Dry milk	1 pint Vanilla ice cream (melted)
2 sleeves Graham crackers (crushed)	1 can Sprite
1 bag Vanilla wafers (crushed and some whole)	

Combine milk, ice cream, cream cheese, and Cool-downs into large bowl. Stir constantly while adding Sprite (a little at a time) until a thick and creamy consistency is achieved. Set aside.

Crush graham crackers and mold in a large bowl (as the crust) on the bottom and sides using a small amount of Sprite stirred into the graham crackers to help adhere to sides of bowl. Don't get too wet!

Pour the mixture into the crust. Crush all the Vanilla wafers, (except enough whole wafers to cover the top of cheesecake). Sprinkle the crushed wafers on top of the filling and then cover these with one layer of whole wafers.

Cover and let set for about 4 hours. Drink remaining Sprite.

Serves: 8

DID YOU KNOW? Cashew nut shells contain oil that is extremely irritating to human skin.

Let's Try Key Lime Pie

1 can Strawberry-Kiwi juice	5 packets Lemon Cool-downs
1 Lemon/lime sports drink	2 bags Dry milk
8 packets Sweeteners	5 packets Cream cheese
1 package Vanilla cookies (separate filling and crush)	

Separate cookies and scrape cream into an insert cup. Place cookies in a large bowl and crush. Mix crushed cookies with 6 spoonfuls of water and form into a crust.

In the insert cup, combine milk, sweeteners, lemon Cool-downs, and 2 packets cream cheese with juice. Pour the juice in a little at a time. (You will have some left over.) Stir until smooth. You do not want it to be runny. Pour into crust. Let set a couple of hours.

In your insert cup, combine 3 packets cream cheese, cookie cream, and sports drink until it is creamy. Heat in hot pot for about 15 minutes and stir well. Spread over pie and let set another few hours.

Serves: 6

SUBSTITUTE: If you want a lemon pie that is not as "tart" as the Key Lime, only use 2 packets of the Lemon-cool-downs in the milk mixture and use a Sprite in place of the Strawberry-Kiwi juice. And then, only use ½ packet of the Cool-down with the cream filling.

> **DID YOU KNOW?** The U. S. Army packs Tabasco pepper sauce in every ration kit that they give to soldiers.

Lotsa Lemon Pudding

1 bag Vanilla wafers (crushed ½)	1 bag Dry milk
1 packet Lemon Cool-down	2 packets Sweeteners
1 can Sprite	

In a large bowl, crush half (½) the Vanilla wafers. Add milk, Cool-down, and sweeteners. Slowly add Sprite while continuously stirring. You will not use the entire can. Continue stirring until thick and creamy.

In another large bowl, line bottom and sides with Vanilla wafers. Pour in enough filling to cover and add another layer of wafers. Alternate with filling and wafers until everything is gone.

Let set for 2 hours. Drink the rest of the soda while waiting.

Serves: 6

> **DID YOU KNOW?** Sweetbread is neither sweet, nor bread. It is a dish made up of the pancreas of the thymus gland of a colt or lamb.

Love That Lemon Cheesecake

1 packet Lemon Cool-down	1 package Bud's Best Lemon cookies (crushed)
1 pint Lemon Swirl ice cream	2 bags Dry milk
12 packets Cream cheese	Water
1 package Lemon cream cookies (separated and crushed)	

Let ice cream melt in container. Separate cookies and place filling in an insert cup and the cookies in a large bowl. Heat cream filling in hot pot for 30 minutes.

Crush the cookies. Lightly crush the bag of Bud's cookies (leave in bag). Add ¾ of these to the crushed cookies in the bowl. Add a little water (a spoonful at a time) until you can form it into a dough. Press into the bottom and sides of the bowl to form a crust.

In another large bowl, add the melted ice cream, Cool-down, and 10 of the cream cheese packets. Add the milk, while stirring continuously. You do no want any lumps. Use all the milk. You can add a little water, if needed for a creamy consistency. Do not let it get runny. Pour into crust and let set at least 3 hours.

Add the last 2 cream cheese packets to the cream filling and mix well. Spread on top of cheesecake after it is set. Finely crush remaining cookies (in bag) and sprinkle over top.

Let set 1 hour.

Serves: 6

DID YOU KNOW? In America, pepperoni is the favorite pizza topping and anchovies always ranks last.

Macaroon Cookie Sandwiches

1 package Macaroon cookies	1 package Trail mix (crushed)
1 Chick-O-Stick (crushed)	Water
1 package Cream cookies (any flavor, remove filling and crush)	

Filling: Remove cream filling and place inside insert cup and heat until melted. Stir in a little water to make it creamy. Stir in Trail mix and Chick-O-Stick.

Spread mixture on 16 cookies and then top with the remaining 16 cookies.

Serves: 8

VARIATION: Add 1 teaspoon of hot chocolate drink mix or coffee, depending on what flavor of cookies used.

DID YOU KNOW? The banana plant can grow as high as 20 feet tall. That's as tall as a 2-story house!

Molten Lava Cake

4 packets Cream cheese	1 package Chocolate covered peanuts
½ bottle Strawberry preserves	2 Hershey's plain candy bar
1 packet Double Fudge cookies (separate and crush)	

Separate cookies and place cream filling in an insert cup and place the cookies in a large bowl.

Crush cookies. Add a little water (a spoonful at a time) and form into dough. Flatten dough into a rectangle of a large chip bag. Press chocolate covered peanuts into dough. Spread jam evenly on top.

Add cream cheese and Hershey's to filling. Melt in hot pot and mix well. Spread over the jam. Roll into a log and carefully place in a large chip bag. Make sure and double bag! Cook for at least an hour. Serve warm. **This is a hit!**

Serves: 8

DID YOU KNOW? Caffeine: There are 100 to 150 milligrams of caffeine in an 8 ounce cup of brewed coffee; 10 milligrams in a 6 ounce cup of cocoa; 5 to 10 milligrams in 1 ounce of bittersweet chocolate; and 5 milligrams in 1 ounce of milk chocolate.

New Yorker Cheesecake

10 packets Cream cheese	3 bags Dry milk
1 package Vanilla cream cookies (remove filling & crush)	1 can Sprite

Remove filling from the cookies and place in insert cup and set aside. In a large bowl, crush cookies for crust. Add just enough water to mix cookies into a crust on the bottom and sides of the bowl.

In an insert cup, add the cream filling and cream cheese. Add about 3 tablespoons of Sprite. Heat until melted together.

In another large bowl, add milk and Sprite (a little at a time), stirring constantly to remove all lumps. Keep the consistency thick.

When the lumps are removed, add the cream cheese and filling mixture. Stir until well blended. Add a little more Sprite, if needed. Pour filling into crust and let set for 4 hours. **Watch out Big Apple!**

Serves: 6

DID YOU KNOW? Astronaut John Glenn ate the first meal in space when he ate pureed applesauce squeezed from a tube aboard the Friendship 7 in 1962.

One Muddy Cake

1 pint Strawberry ice cream (for strawberries)	5 Banana Moon pies
2 Nutzo ice cream bars (remove the cones & crush)	1 pint Rocky Road ice cream (melted)
1 Hershey's plain candy bar (melted in wrapper)	1 bag Vanilla wafers

Break up Moon pies into bite size pieces and set aside in a large bowl. In another large bowl, line it with whole Vanilla wafers. Make sure to go up the sides of the bowl.

In another bowl, mix together the Rocky Road ice cream, and just the ice cream from the 2 Nutzos. Crush the Nutzo cones into the Moon pies and pour into ice cream mixture and blend well. Then pour over crust spreading evenly.

Dump the Strawberry ice cream into another bowl and remove the strawberries. Place the strawberries on top of cake. Melt the Hershey's bar (in its wrapper) in the hot pot. Cut off end of wrapper and drizzle over cake. Let set about 2 hours.

Eat the Strawberry ice cream while waiting for the cake to set.

Serves: 6

DID YOU KNOW? The first soup was made of hippopotamus. The earliest archeological evidence for the consumption of soup dates back to 6000 BC, and it was hippopotamus soup!

Oven Free Oatmeal Chocolate Cookies

40 packets Sweeteners	½ cup Dry milk
6 tablespoons Butter	½ cup Peanut butter
½ cup Hot chocolate drink mix	8 packages Oatmeal (any flavor)

Combine the sweetener, butter, hot chocolate, and dry milk in a large cooking bag and heat until everything is dissolved into the melted butter.

Stir in peanut butter (mixture will be thick). Then, add oatmeal (dry). It is easier to mix if you squeeze bag continually.

Drop the mixture by the spoonfuls onto typing paper (or a clean chip bag) and flatten to resemble baked cookies. Allow cookies to firm up (about 1 hour).

Serves: 4

VARIATION: Use all plain oatmeal and break up a Hershey's plain candy bar into small pieces and mix in at same time as the oatmeal. Or, add a package of M&Ms plain candy without nuts. Or, add nuts, too. You might forget you are in prison while you're eating them! **Yummy!**

DID YOU KNOW? There is a company in Taiwan that makes dinnerware out of wheat, so you can eat your plate!

Party Time

2 packages Duplex cookies (separated and crushed)	8 Oatmeal cream pies
1 package Bud's Best Butterfinger cookies (crushed)	2 Chick-O-Sticks
2 Snickers candy bars (broken apart)	3 Rice Krispy Treats
1 Hershey's plain candy bar (melted in wrapper)	4 Nutty bars (twin packs)
½ cup Hot chocolate drink mix	2 tablespoons Peanut butter
1 M&Ms plain candies (crushed)	Water

Separate cream from cookies and place the cookies in a large bowl and crush. Put filling in an insert cup and set aside. Add about 8 tablespoons of hot water to the cookies and mix together until it is the consistency of dough. Form crust to the bottom and sides of the bowl, reserving just enough to make a top layer. The crust will only go about halfway up the bowl.

In another bowl, pour in the hot chocolate and add enough water to make it thick. Break up 1 Rice Krispy Treat and add the peanut butter and mix well. It will be thick. Pour into crust and top with crushed Butterfinger cookies. Press these into the dough with your spoon to cover up the filling.

In another large bowl, (break into pieces) the 5 Oatmeal pies, 2 Rice Krispy Treats, and 2 Nutty bars. Combine and mix well. Then pour these on top of the second layer. Take the remaining cookie dough and cover the top like a pie.

Let set for 1 hour, than flip over on a chip bag. Add 1 teaspoon of hot water to the cream filling. Stir until it becomes icing and then spread on top. Decorate with the M&Ms and Snickers. Melt the Hershey bar (in it's wrapper) in hot pot. Cut corner off of Hershey bar and drizzle over top of candy. **Delicious and a real treat!**

Serves: 6-8

DID YOU KNOW? They have square watermelons in Japan. They stack better.

Peanut Butter Cookie Drops

12 Chick-O-Sticks (crushed)	4 Milky Way candy bars
2 teaspoons Peanut Butter	1 Hershey's plain candy bar
1 bag Bud's Best Butterfinger Cookies	

In an insert cup, break up the candy bars and combine with the peanut butter and stir well until all is melted and creamy.

In a large bowl, combine the crushed cookies and Chick-O-Sticks. Stir well. Add the melted candy bars and combine well. Drop by teaspoonful's onto a large (empty) chip bag. Let set for at least 1 hour.

Serves: 4

DID YOU KNOW? 50% of pizzas in America are pepperoni.

Peanut/Chocolate Cream Cookies

¼ cup Hot chocolate drink mix	1 Nutty bar (twin pack)
1 tablespoon Peanut butter	8 Vanilla wafers (crushed)
1 tablespoon Hot water	

In a large bowl, combine hot chocolate, peanut butter, and hot water until smooth, and creamy. Crush the Nutty bars and add just 2 crushed wafers to make it thick and mix well. Place on one Vanilla wafer and then top with another one.

Serves: 1

VARIATION: Substitute Vanilla wafer's for any type of cookie. Also, this spread can be used to top a cheesecake, too.

DID YOU KNOW? It has been traditional to serve fish with a slice of lemon since the Middle Ages, because it was believed that the fruit's juice would dissolve any bones accidentally swallowed.

Root Beer Float Cake

1 package Cinnamon donuts	1 can Root Beer soda
1 Butterfinger candy bar (crushed)	1 package Vanilla cookies (separate and crush)

In a large bowl, combine crushed cookies with about 6 spoonfuls of Root Beer. Form into a crust on the cookie's plastic wrapper (that is completely opened to form a large rectangle). The crust will be about 6" by 9". Make an edge that is about a finger width high around the entire crust.

In the large bowl, mix the cream filling with about 2 spoonfuls of Root Beer and spread over cake. Crush donuts and sprinkle over filling. Lightly push down so they stick to the filling. Top with the crushed Butterfinger. Let set at least 1 hour. Drink the remaining Root Beer while you are waiting.

Serves: 6

SUBSTITUTE: Try using 3 Chick-O-Sticks in place of the Butterfinger candy bars if you don't want the chocolate taste. Using Big Red in place of the Root Beer makes a sweeter cake if you want a change. Or, for Christmas or Valentines, too.

DID YOU KNOW? The English word "soup" comes from the middle ages word "sop", which means a slice of bread over which roast drippings were poured.

Root Beer Float on the River Pie

2 packets Cream cheese	1 package Cinnamon donuts (crushed)
1 can Root Beer	2 Chick-O-Sticks (crushed)
1 package Vanilla cream cookies (separate & crush)	

Separate cookies from the filling and crush cookies in a large bowl. To the cookies, add 8 tablespoons of Root Beer. Mix until the crust is pliable. Press into bottom and sides of the bowl and remove about ½ inch from around the top edges to use on top of filling.

Stir 3 tablespoons of Root Beer with the cream filling and cream cheese in a separate bowl. Stir until mixture is smooth and creamy. Pour and spread over the crust.

Sprinkle the donuts on top of the filling mixture. Press the cookie edges into the donuts. Then, sprinkle Chick-O-Sticks on the very top. Let set for 1 hour.

Serves: 6

VARIATION: Try using Big Red instead of the Root Beer for a pink delight, or Big Blue, too. And, use powdered donuts in place of the cinnamon with this change.

DID YOU KNOW? Brown lentils are slightly larger than red or fancy black. They are ideal for sautéing because they are less likely to fall apart when crisped in the skillet.

Smolé

1 bag Pork skins	2 Hershey's plain candy bars
1 row Chocolate cream cookies (separate and crush)	

Separate filling from cookies. Place filling in an insert cup with candy bars. Heat until melted, stirring continuously.

In a bowl, crush cookies. Set aside.

Dip one end of the pork skin into the melted chocolate. Then, dip into crushed cookies. Set on a chip bag to harden. Repeat process until everything is gone. **Surprisingly addictive!**

Serves: 3-4 as a snack

DID YOU KNOW? The World's first chocolate candy was produced in 1828 by Dutch chocolate-maker Conrad J. Van Houten. He pressed the fat from roasted cocoa beans to produce cocoa butter, in which he added cocoa powder and sugar.

Snickeroonies

3 Snickers candy bars	2 bags Dry milk
3 Nutty bars (twin pack crushed)	2 packages Peanuts
3 tablespoons Hot chocolate drink mix	Water
1 package Vanilla cream cookies (separated & crushed)	

Separate cream from cookies and place each in separate large bowls.

Crush the cookies. Make sure they are finely crushed with no lumps. Add enough water to form into dough. Don't let it get too wet. Form into a crust on the bottom and sides of the bowl.

Add Nutty bars, hot chocolate, and peanuts to the cream filling. Add just enough water to make the mixture creamy. Mix well. Set aside.

Place Snickers into hot pot insert (leave inside wrapper) and add just enough water so that they will melt as they are heating. When completely melted, add the dry milk to the filling mixture and squeeze the melted Snickers into the mixture. Stir this while adding enough water to form a thick pancake-like batter. Pour into the crust.

Let set at least 6 hours until firm.

Serves: 6

SUBSTITUTE: Try using Milky Ways or 3-Musketeers for anyone that does not want nuts. It's a creamy sensation.

DID YOU KNOW? Ketchup was originally created as a drug, not a condiment.

Strawberry Cheesecake

4 packages Dry milk	1 Hershey's plain candy bar
1 can Strawberry soda	1 bag Vanilla wafers
Water	

Crust: Crush Vanilla wafers in a large bowl. Add a few spoonful's of water, a little at a time, to form crust on bottom and up the sides of the bowl.

Filling: In another large bowl, pour in 3 of the milk packages. Pour in the strawberry soda, a little at a time, constantly stirring to remove lumps. You don't want it too runny, so use sparingly. If it's too runny add more milk. You need to stir this for a long time (until your arm aches). Keep adding milk or soda (as needed) until all of the milk is used. When fluffy, pour into crust and cover for several hours.

When ready to serve, melt candy bar in hot pot (leave in wrapper). Cut corner off wrapper and swirl over the top of cheesecake.

Serves: 6

DID YOU KNOW? In Japan, the most popular pizza topping is squid.

Strawberry/Cherry Cheesecake

1 pint Strawberry/Vanilla ice cream (melted & remove strawberries & cut into small pieces)	1 package Duplex cookies (separate and crush)
3 bags Dry milk	2 Cherry pies (remove fillings)
2 packets Cream cheese	12 packets Sweeteners

Separate cookies and put cream into an insert. Place cookies in a large bowl and crush. Mix crushed cookies with 6 spoonfuls of water. Form into a crust on the bottom and up the sides of the bowl.

Separate filling from pies and place in insert cup, and set aside. Crumble cherry pie crust over cookie crust and spread it out. Press this into cookie crust.

In another bowl combine milk, sweeteners, ice cream (remove strawberries and set aside). Then, stir well until thick and creamy. You may have to add a little water to reach desired consistency. Don't get too runny. Cut up strawberry pieces and add. Stir until mixed well. Pour into crust. After it sets about an hour, prepare topping.

Topping: In hot pot insert, combine cream cheese and cream fillings. Heat for about 30 minutes. Then add the cherry pie fillings and mix well. Spread over cheesecake.

Serves: 6

DID YOU KNOW? Bananas aren't fruit! They are a type of herb. They are in the same family as lilies, orchids and palms.

Strawberry Jelly Roll

4 packets Cream cheese	½ bottle Strawberry preserves
1 package Cream cookies (any flavor) (separate filling and crush)	

Separate cream from cookies and place cookies in a large bowl. Store in cookie wrapper for future use. Crush cookies and add a little water, to form into a dough. Add cream cheese and blend well. Spread out on an empty chip bag to form a rectangle about ½ inch thick. Spread jam evenly on top leaving a 1½ inch space around all the sides. Roll into a log.

Place inside the chip bag and heat in hot pot. After about 30-45 minutes, remove from chip bag and cut.

Serves: 6

VARIATION: Sprinkle crushed nuts on top of preserves before rolling. Drizzle a melted Hershey's plain candy bar over the jam, if you need more sugar. Or, press a bag of chocolate covered peanuts into the dough, before spreading the jam on top, if you want to go all out.

DID YOU KNOW? Research shows that only 43% of homemade dinners served in the U. S. includes vegetables.

Strawberry Shortcake Cheeseballs

1 pint Strawberry ice cream (melted)	4 packets Cream cheese
2 bags Dry milk	Water
1 package Vanilla cream cookies (crushed whole)	

Let ice cream melt leaving it in container. In a large bowl, crush the entire cookie into a fine powder and set aside.

In another large bowl, pour in ice cream, cream cheese, and both milks. Add 2 teaspoons of water. Stir until thick and creamy. Add a little more water, if needed, you don't want it runny. Let set for 2-3 hours.

When set, with spoon, scoop cheesecake into small balls. Roll in cookie powder and set on a large chip bag. **These are so delicious!**

Serves: 6-8

> **DID YOU KNOW?** The average American drinks about 600 sodas a year.

Suckers

5 Popsicle sticks	5 packets Cool-downs (various flavors)
1 bag Pasqual candies (separate colors and crush)	

Slam the candy (in the wrapper) on the concrete floor to break it up. Separate each color into small chip bags to melt. Put all the bags at the same time in the hot pot to melt. Sprinkle a Cool-down into each bag for a little tartness. When candy is hot and melted, mold into a sucker. Push popsicle stick into sucker while it's still hot. Cool on the chip bags. **Clever!**

Serves: 5

> **DID YOU KNOW?** Popcorn's nutritional value comes from the fact that, like other cereal grains, it's primary function is to provide the body with heat and energy.

Super Surprise

1 bag Plain potato chips (crushed)	8 Maria's cookies
2 teaspoons Salad dressing	

Spread salad dressing evenly on 4 cookies. Sprinkle crushed chips on top to cover salad dressing. Top with another cookie. Repeat 3 times.

Surprisingly easy and very tasty!

Serves: 1

> **DID YOU KNOW?** Eskimo ice cream is not icy or creamy.

Sweet Banana Pudding

1 pint Banana Pudding ice cream (melted)	2 Banana Fudge ice cream bars (melted)
8 packets Sweeteners	6 Banana Moon pies (crumble into pieces)
1 bag Vanilla wafers (set aside ½)	½ bag Dry milk
1 package Banana Whey (add water according to package)	

In a large bowl, combine ice cream, fudge bars, and whey. Stir well. In another large bowl, combine milk and sweeteners with enough water to make into a thick pudding. (Remember the longer it sets the thicker it will get). Set aside.

In another large bowl, form a layer of cookies in bottom and up the sides. Add about 1/3 of the crumbled Moon pies. Pour in some of the pudding and repeat with the cookie, Moon pies, then liquid, until you have used everything.

Crush some wafers over the top. Let set a few hours.

Serves: 4

SUBSTITUTE: 1 sleeve of Graham crackers can be used in place of the Vanilla wafers.

DID YOU KNOW? The onion is the vegetable that ancient Egyptian's placed their right hand on when taking an oath. Its round shape symbolized eternity.

The Fence Hoppers

1 Milky Way candy bar	2 Mint sticks (crushed)
1 package Chocolate cream cookies (crushed whole)	Water

In a large bowl, crush the entire cookie (reserve the plastic tray the cookies came in). Crush the mint sticks (separately) into fine powder. Add 1 mint stick to the crushed cookies and mix well. Then, add a spoonful of water at a time, mixing well until the cookies are formed into dough.

Divide equally into 3 parts. Press each one into 1 row in the plastic container. Each row will be filled to the top.

In an insert cup, place the Milky Way and other mint stick. Mix well. When melted, pour into each of the 3 rows equally. Let set for 2 hours. Cut each row in half.

Serves: 6

DID YOU KNOW? Fried chicken is the most popular meal ordered in sit-down restaurants in the U.S. The next in popularity are: Roast beef, spaghetti, turkey, baked ham, and fried shrimp.

There is a Nut Cake in the Pen

1 Milky Way candy bar	1 package Peanuts (crushed)
2 Snickers candy bars	Water
1 package Vanilla cream cookies (separate and crush)	

Separate cream filling from cookies and place in insert cup. Put cookies in large bowl.

Break up the candy bars and crush the candy bars into the cream filling. Heat until everything is melted. Mix well. Stir in peanuts.

Crush the cookies and leave lumpy. Add water, a little at a time, until it is the consistency of dough. Transfer to a large chip bag.

Pour the insert cup mixture over the cookie dough and squeeze the bag until everything is combined. Place inside another chip bag and heat in hot pot for another 30 minutes.

When done, divide into 6 bowls and eat warm! **Delicious!**

Serves: 6

SUBSTITUTE: If you are a chocolate lover try using Double Fudge cookies for the ultimate experience. Or, try chocolate cream cookies for a milder yet still chocolate taste. You can always substitute sunflower seeds for the peanuts.

DID YOU KNOW? Swiss Steak, Chop Suey, and Russian Dressing all originated in the United States.

Tippy's Fave

1 Moon pie (any flavor)	2 Hershey's plain candy bars
1 package Nuts (any kind)	1 M&Ms plain candies (broken into small pieces)

Place unwrapped Moon pie in a large plastic bowl (leave whole). Melt chocolate bars in the hot pot leaving them in their wrappers,

Crush M&Ms and nuts until they are small pieces. Pour on top of Moon pie and then cut open corner of candy bar wrappers and squeeze contents over the Moon pie. It will run down the sides.

Set aside until the chocolate hardens and adheres to the M&Ms and nuts to the Moon pie. Cut in half and share with a friend. **Out of this world!**

Serves: 2

DID YOU KNOW? The sandwich is named for the Fourth Earl of Sandwich (1718-1792), for whom sandwiches were invented, so that he could stay at the gambling table without interruption for meals.

Ultimate Honey Bun Sandwich

2 Honey Buns	1 Milky Way candy bar
1 tablespoon Peanut butter	

Melt candy bar in wrapper in hot pot. When melted, open one end.

Spread peanut butter on top of one honey bun and squeeze Milky Way on top of peanut butter.

Place the other honey bun on top of this. Place in chip bag and heat for 30 minutes.

Cut in half and enjoy with a friend.

Serves: 2

DID YOU KNOW? Vanilla is the extract of fermented and dried pods of several species of orchids.

You'd Be Surprised No File Cake

1 packet Cream cheese	3 packets Sweeteners
2 Fireballs (jaw breakers)	¼ cup Water
1 package Vanilla cream cookies (separate & crush)	

Separate cookies and place filling in an insert cup. Add cream cheese to the cream filling and stir well. (This will be the icing).

In a large bowl, crush cookies into fine powder. Make sure there are no lumps. Add sweeteners to the cookies and mix well. Set aside.

Cook the fireballs in hot pot insert with the water until melted. This will take a while. Stir frequently. Pour into cookies slowly as you mix well. If the mixture is too dry, add a small amount of water.

Place the dough into a bowl and form into a small cake. After it is completely cool, add the icing mixture to the top of the cake, and frost.

Serves: 4

DID YOU KNOW? Although the combination of chili peppers and oregano for seasoning has been traced to the ancient Aztecs, the present blend is said to be the invention of early Texans. Chili powder today is typically a blend of dried chilies, garlic powder, red peppers, oregano, and cumin.

You'll Not Want to Share Pie

6 Oatmeal pies	4 packets Cream cheese
2 bags Dry milk	1 Hershey's plain candy bar (melted)
1 Milky Way candy bar	Water
1 pint Pralines & Cream ice cream (melted)	

Let ice cream melt in container. In a large bowl, break apart oatmeal pies. Press them into bottom of bowl and up the sides to form a crust.

In another bowl, add the melted ice cream and cream cheese. Add milk, a little at a time, while continuously stirring. You want to use all the milk. Keep stirring until there are no lumps and it's thick and creamy. Add a little water, if needed. Do not get too runny.

Pour into crust. Break up the Milky Way into small pieces and drop into filling. Spread the filling evenly into crust.

Let set 2-3 hours. Just before serving, melt Hershey's (leaving in wrapper). Cut off corner of the wrapper and drizzle over pie.

Scrumptious!

Serves: 6

DID YOU KNOW? In the 1920s, William Murrie who later became the president of Hershey, tried to convince Hershey that they should produce a chocolate bar with peanuts. Hershey didn't like the idea, but let them go ahead as long as the bar wasn't under the Hershey brand name. Thus, in 1925, the "Chocolate Sales Corporation," a fictitious company Murrie came up with, delivered the "Mr. Goodbar," which ended up being wildly successful!

IV
All Holiday's
Treats

Christmas Cookies

Hershey's Kisses

Cookie Cakes

Chocolate
Covered
Cherries

All Holiday's Basic Cookie/Cake Recipe

¼ cup Hot chocolate drink mix	6 tablespoons Water
1 package Cream cookies (any flavor) (separate and crush)	

Separate the cream from the cookies and put cookies in a large bowl to crush. Put cream aside to use in another recipe. (I store it in the wrapper from the cookies.). Crush cookies until they are coarse.

Add the hot chocolate and mix well. Add the water, a little at a time, until you can form the dough into a ball. Be careful not to get too wet. Use in your favorite recipe.

Serves: 1 recipe

JUST A THOUGHT: A real friend is one who walks in when the rest of the world walks out. Marilou Gibbs

All Holiday's Basic Frosting Recipe

2 teaspoons Dry milk	2 packets Cream cheese
1 package Cream cookies (remove filling)	Water

Separate cookies and place cream filling in an insert cup. Add other ingredients and mix well. Heat in hot pot until creamy. Add a little more dry milk if not stiff enough. Add water, if needed.

Keep cookie tops and bottoms in the cookie wrapper and store for future use.

Serves: 1 recipe

VARIATION: One-quarter (¼) piece of a cinnamon candy stick crushed and added to mixture gives an excellent flavor, too.

JUST A THOUGHT: People may forget what you said and they may forget what you did. However, they will never forget how you made them feel. Unknown

All Holiday's Candy Patties

1 package Pasqual candies (separate colors and crush)	1 package Orange slices (cut into small pieces)

Slam candies on concrete floor to crush (leave in wrapper). Separate the candies into colors. Divide orange slices into 4 equal piles.

In an insert cup, add 1 color of candies and 1 of the orange slice piles. Heat, but don't melt all the way. It needs to stick together and remain chewy. It will be round, formed to the bottom of the insert.

Repeat until all 4 patties are made.

Serves: 2

VARIATION: Try using crushed Fireballs, crushed peanuts, crushed mint sticks, or crushed fruit sticks in place of (or in addition to) the orange slices. **Use your imagination!**

JUST A THOUGHT: Only the limits of our mindset can determine the boundaries of our future. Unknown

---

All Holiday's Chocolate Covered Pretzels

1 bag Party Mix (pretzels only)	3 Mint sticks (crushed fine)
1 package Chocolate covered peanuts	

Remove peanuts from the chocolate and melt in an insert cup. Save peanuts to use with another recipe. Store them in the candy package. Dip pretzels into chocolate and place on chip bag to harden. Sprinkle with the mint sticks. Let set until hard. (A dental flosser makes a good tool to dip with).

Serves: 16–20 pretzels

VARIATION: Crush the peanuts and add to chocolate, while melting. (Still sprinkle with the crushed mint sticks).

JUST A THOUGHT: If people were superior to animals, they'd take better care of the world. Winnie the Pooh

---

All Holiday's Nutty Chocolate Treat

1 package Chocolate covered peanuts (softened)

In a hot pot, partially melt chocolate, (just enough to soften, leave in the package). If it is too melted just wait a few minutes before molding it. Let it cool completely before giving it to a friend.

For Valentine's Day: Form into a heart shape.

For St. Patrick's Day: Form a clover. Make sure it has 4 leafs!

For Halloween: Form a pumpkin. Don't forget the stem.

For Christmas: Form a candy cane. Sprinkle with a crushed mint stick before chocolate hardens.

VARIATION: If you don't want nuts, use 4 packages of M&Ms plain or 6 Hershey's plain candy bars. Or, make both with and without nuts.

Serves: 1

> **JUST A THOUGHT:** If you can't say no, then you lose your ability to say "yes". Unknown

Baby Rattles

1 All Holiday's Basic Cookie/Cake recipe	1 All Holiday's Basic Frosting recipe
1 packet Cream cheese	Water
1 M&M's plain candies (separate by colors)	

Place desired color of M&M's into about 1 teaspoon of water to remove color. On an empty chip bag, shape the cookie mixture into a rattle. Make a circle for the top of the rattle. Then, make the handle about 1 inch wide and 3 inches long.

For the bottom of the handle, make a triangle that is hollow in the middle. Pour the colored water into the frosting and mix well. Add the cream cheese and continue to mix well. Spread on top of cake.

Serves: 6

TOPPING IDEAS: Use crushed M&Ms, crushed mint sticks, or crushed Chick-O-Sticks and sprinkle over the top of the rattle.

> **JUST A THOUGHT:** One of the most striking differences between a cat and a lie is that a cat has only nine lives. Mark Twain

Christmas Candy Canes & Stockings

1 bag Chocolate peanuts (remove peanuts & melt)	1 packet Cream cheese
1 All Holiday's Basic Cookie/Cake recipe	1 Cream filling from cookies
1 M&Ms plain candies (need red only)	1 Mint stick (crushed)

Prepare All Holiday's Basic Cookie/Cake recipe. Flatten the dough out on a large chip bag to make cookie shapes.

Form dough into candy cane shapes and stocking shapes. On the back of each piece, spread layer of melted chocolate. Hershey's bars do not harden as well as the chocolate covered peanuts. Let harden with chocolate side facing up. When hard, turn over because dough side is the top.

In hot pot insert, combine cream cheese with the cream filling. Save half to make red. Make stiff to cover candy cane, so don't add too much water.

Drop red M&Ms in about a teaspoonful of water to remove color. Mix color into filling. Add crushed mint stick. Put stripes on with the red filling mixture.

Make sure the stockings have chocolate side down. Place white frosting on top and red frosting on the bottom of the stocking. Use very stiff red in a small chip bag to write names on the stocking. These are really cute!

Serves: 6-8

> **JUST A THOUGHT:** Very little is needed to make a happy life; it is all within yourself, in your way of thinking. Marcus Aurelius

Christmas Cocoa

1 tablespoon Irish Cream cappuccino	2 tablespoons Hot chocolate drink mix
2 packets Sweeteners	Water
1 Mint Stick (crushed)	

Pour all ingredients into hot pot insert. Add hot water and stir well. Heat in hot pot until the mixture is dissolved. Transfer to your mug. Relax and listen to the holiday music on your radio.

Double the recipe and share with your b.f.

Serves: 1

> **JUST A THOUGHT:** Always be a first rate version of yourself rather than a second rate version of someone else. Unknown

Christmas Holiday Squares

2 Nutty bars (twin pack) (crushed)	1 All Holiday's Basic Cookie/Cake recipe
2 packets Cream cheese	1 M&Ms plain candies (crushed)
1 Hershey's plain candy bar (melted in wrapper)	

Use All Holiday's Basic Cookie/Cake recipe and form into 1½" squares on an open, empty chip bag. Let squares set for almost an hour.

In hot pot, melt chocolate (leaving it in the wrapper). Cut off corner and squeeze over squares. Let set until it hardens.

In a large bowl, combine crushed Nutty bars with cream cheese. Spread generous amount over each square and top with crushed M&Ms.

Serves: 4

JUST A THOUGHT: Nothing is predestined: The obstacles of your past can become the gateways that lead to new beginnings. Unknown

Christmas Mint Cookies

1 package Chocolate cream cookies	3 Mint sticks
1 packet Cream cheese	1 teaspoon Water

Take filling out of cookies and set cookies aside. Keep the cookies whole. Break up mint sticks and place in an insert cup with a teaspoon of water. Heat in hot pot to melt completely (this will take a few hours). When melted, add cream cheese and mix well. Place the mixture back between the cookies.

Serves: Makes 32 cookies

VARIATION: I like to melt Hershey's candy bars and spread over the top of the finished cookie. Let set about 30 minutes for the chocolate to re-harden. For even a more "minty" flavor-crush a mint stick and sprinkle on top of the melted Hershey's. **It's festive!**

JUST A THOUGHT: Anger is not a natural emotion. It is not found in animals. All our anger is based upon fear. Unknown

Christmas Rudolph

2 Hershey's plain candy bars	4 Fireball jaw breakers
4 Oatmeal cookies	4 Pretzel's (break in half) (from Party Mix)

Place the 4 cookies on an empty chip bag. Leave candy bars in wrapper and melt in hot pot. After melted, cut corner off one end of wrapper.

Adhere the pretzel "antlers" to the cookie by using the chocolate as "glue". Use the chocolate to make eyes and mouth. The fireball is for his nose-adhere with chocolate. **Very Cute!**

Serves: 4

JUST A THOUGHT: Circumstances are beyond human control, but our conduct is in our own power. Benjamin Disreli

---

Christmas Snowman

5 Rice Crispy Treats	1 M&Ms plain candies
1 packet Cream cheese	1 All Holiday's Basic Frosting recipe
4 Hershey's plain candy bars (melted)	

Leave candy bars in wrapper and melt in hot pot. Place M&Ms (by color) in about a teaspoonful of water to remove color. Pour into frosting (in a small chip bag), and blend well. Cut one corner off the bag so that it makes an easy icing bag.

Make 2 balls out each of 4 Rice Crispy bars. Use the 5th bar to make a hat for your snowman. Make bottom ball slightly bigger and put them together. Squeeze the colored filling around middle of snowman to resemble a belt. Cut one corner off the bottom of the candy bar. Use melted chocolate for eyes, nose, and mouth. Attach the hat with melted chocolate. **Precious!**

Serves: 4

JUST A THOUGHT: You can never cross the ocean unless you have the courage to lose sight of the shore. Christopher Columbus

---

Christmas Tree Bark

4 Mint sticks (crushed)	1 package Chocolate covered peanuts
1 package Graham crackers (broken into sections)	

Remove peanuts from chocolate and set aside to use in another recipe. Store the nuts in the candy package. Melt chocolate in an insert cup.

Cover top of graham crackers with melted chocolate. Sprinkle with the crushed mint sticks. Let set until hard.

Serves: 8

JUST A THOUGHT: No one can put you down without your consent! Red Bootz

Cinco de Mayo S'Mores

1 Hershey's plain candy bar	2 Chocolate Moon pies
2 Flour tortilla's	1 teaspoon Butter
1 package Cinnamon donuts	

Scrape all of the cinnamon sugar off the donuts into a bowl. Spread the butter evenly over the 2 flour tortillas and sprinkle both with the cinnamon sugar.

Remove the marshmallow from the Moon pies and place on each tortilla. Break up the candy bar and place ½ on top of each marshmallow. Fold the tortilla in half and place in a large cooking bag.

Cook in hot pot for about 45 minutes. Serve warm. **Delicious!**

Serves: 2

JUST A THOUGHT: Great minds think alike, fools seldom differ. Unknown

Cinco de Mayo Suckers

1 package Pascual candies (crushed)	1 packet Lemon Cool-down
5 Popsicle sticks	1 packet Chili soup seasoning

Leave the candy in the wrapper and slam it on the concrete floor to break it up. Unwrap and place the candies in a large bowl. Add the chili seasoning and Cool-down and mix well.

Then, pour everything into a large chip bag and cook in hot pot until melted. Shape into 5 suckers and push in the popsicle stick. It's easier to shape each sucker inside a flour tortilla bag because it's more pliable.

Serves: 5

Easter Eggs

4 Rice Crispy Treats (remove candy chips)	1 M&Ms plain candies (for coloring)
Cream filling from cookies	1 packet Cream cheese
Water	1 Milky Way candy bar

Press 2 Rice Crispy's flat and then combine and shape into an egg shape. Set on opened wrapper it came in. Repeat for the second egg.

Cut 1/3 of the top of the egg off to make a lid. Hollow out the center of the egg. Open top and put in half of a candy bar in each egg and close shut.

Combine filling with cream cheese and use M&Ms to make desired color.

To make color: Put 1 spoonful of water in cup and drop M&Ms in to take color off. When color is removed, take out M&Ms and eat! Add colored water to cream filling and mix well. Put dots of colored filling on egg and put small candy pieces in center to decorate. To easily make dots, put the filling into a small chip bag. Cut off one corner and use as an icing bag.

Serves: 2

> **JUST A THOUGHT:** The weak can never forgive. Forgiveness is the attribute of the strong. Unknown

---

4th of July Flag

1 All Holiday's Basic/Cookie Cake recipe	1 All Holiday's Basic Frosting recipe
1 packet Cream cheese	1-2 tablespoons Dry milk
1 M&M's plain candy	Water

On a large chip bag, make 8 rectangle shapes about ¾ inch thick out of the cake recipe. To the frosting recipe, stir in the cream cheese and milk to make frosting "stiff".

Soak red and blue M&Ms (separately) in about 1 spoonful of water for each color to remove color. Divide frosting into 3 small chip bags. Put more in 1 bag (this will be left white). Pour the red and blue colored water in the other 2 (separately). Add a little dry milk if it's too runny. Frost cakes entirely with white first.

Cut a small hole in 1 corner of each bag. Make a blue square in upper left corner. Alternate red and white for stripes. Use the white to put "dots" inside the blue for stars. **Patriotic!**

Serves: 8

> **JUST A THOUGHT:** Whether you think you can or think you can't; either way you are right. Henry Ford

---

Halloween Candy Corn Squares

1 package Candy corn	1 M&Ms plain candies
1 All Holiday's Basic Cookie/Cake recipe	

Make all Holiday's Basic Cookie/Cake recipe and form into squares about ½" thick and 1" by 1 ½" square.

Place on a large chip bag. (That is opened all the way).

Break candy corn into small pieces and melt completely in an insert cup. This will take a few hours to melt. When melted, pour a small amount over each of the squares (enough to cover). Let set and place M&Ms on top. They are better the next day. **Enjoy!**

Serves: 6

JUST A THOUGHT: To taste the sweetness of life, you must have the power to forget the past. Carrie Dosi – U.K.

Halloween Cookie Pops

1 All Holiday's Basic Cookie/Cake recipe	1 All Holiday's Basic Frosting recipe
1 M&Ms plain candies (desired colors)	20 Q-tips (remove cotton from both ends)
1 package Chocolate covered peanuts (remove nuts and crush)	

By hand, separate the chocolate from the peanuts and place the chocolate only into an insert cup. In a bowl, crush the nuts. Heat chocolate in hot pot until melted.

Roll the prepared cookie mix into about 20 one-to-one-half (1-1½) inch balls. Make an indention in each one with your little finger.

Spoon chocolate into the small hole and insert the Q-tip while it's still soft and stiff enough to hold the stick upright.

Lightly coat the ball with frosting and roll carefully in the crushed nuts.

Serves: 20 (pieces)

VARIATION: Instead of the nuts, try using crushed Chick-O-Sticks, M&Ms, mint sticks, hot chocolate drink mix, or even cappuccino powder. Decorate however you want. You can even put a cute smiley face on your ball. **Have Fun!**

JUST A THOUGHT: To acquire love… fill yourself up with it until you become a magnet. Charles Haanel

---

Halloween Cookie Pops 2

2 Hershey's plain candy bars	1 packet Orange sports drink
1 All Holiday's Basic Frosting recipe	1 package Q-tips (stick only)
1 All Holiday's Basic Cookie/Cake recipe	

Leave candy bars in wrappers and melt in hot pot. Roll 1 inch balls out of the Cookie/Cake mixture, and place on an empty chip bag.

In the frosting mixture, stir in a little of the sports drink and mix well to make the frosting orange. Just remember the more sports drink you use, the more tart it will be. Frost the balls.

Remove the cotton from the Q-tips and push sticks into balls. Cut the corner off 1 side of the candy bars. Squirt a little chocolate into hole and replace stick. Chocolate will keep stick in hole after chocolate hardens. Make faces with the melted chocolate and have fun!

Serves: 6

VARIATION: Crush 5 Chick-O-Sticks, roll the balls in after they are frosted. Or, use M&Ms to make faces or colorful dots. Just let your imagination run wild!

JUST A THOUGHT: If you believe, you will receive whatever you ask for in prayer. Matthew 21:12

Halloween Pumpkin Cake

1 All Holiday's Basic Cookie/Cake recipe	1 All Holiday's Basic Frosting recipe
1 Hershey's plain candy bar	1 packet Orange sports drink
1 package Chocolate covered peanuts	

On a large chip bag, shape the cookie dough into the shape of a pumpkin without a stem. Leave the chocolate covered peanuts inside their package and lightly warm them in a pot to soften them, and then mold them into the shape of a stem. Attach stem to pumpkin while stem is still soft.

Heat the frosting in an insert cup. Stir in the sports drink, a little at a time, to make the shade of orange you want. Too much will make it tart. Spread evenly over pumpkin.

Leave the candy bar in the wrapper and melt in hot pot. When melted, cut corner off of wrapper and squeeze out to make eyes, nose, and mouth. **Cute!**

Serves: 6

JUST A THOUGHT: Every job is a self-portrait of the person who performs it. Unknown

Halloween Pumpkin Cake 2

2 Hershey's plain candy bars	1 package Chocolate covered peanuts
4 packets Cream cheese	2 packets Orange sports drink
1 package Orange slices (cut up)	Water
2 packages Vanilla cream cookies (separate and crush)	

Separate cream from cookies and place cookies in separate large bowl. Add cream cheese and mix well. Set aside. I like to heat the cookie filling in an insert cup for about 30 minutes so it's easier to blend into the cream cheese.

Cut orange slices into pieces and place in an insert cup. Heat until melted. This will take a while. Once melted, add to cream mixture and mix until well blended.

In a cup, fill ½ full with hot water. Add orange sports drink. Stir until dissolved. Set aside.

Crush the cookies. Add flavored water, a spoonful at a time, until the cookies are a firm dough. Mold into a pumpkin on a large chip bag. Leave enough room for a stem on chip bag. Add a spoonful, or two, of flavored water into icing mixture and stir well. Spread over pumpkin.

Lightly melt chocolate covered peanuts in the bag. Mold into a stem and put on top of pumpkin before chocolate hardens.

Melt Hershey's (in their wrappers). When melted, cut off one end of wrapper. Squeeze out chocolate to make eyes, nose, and mouth.

Let set for 3 hours. **Boo!**

Serves: 8-10

JUST A THOUGHT: We don't get over grief. We get through it. Unknown

---

Halloween Pumpkin Candy

1 package Orange slices (tear into small pieces)	2 Hershey's with almonds

Remove almonds from candy bars and set aside. Put the chocolate in a small chip bag and heat in hot pot to melt.

In an insert cup, heat the orange slices until they are pliable and easy to form into pumpkin shapes. While still warm, push the almonds from the Hershey's into the top for the stem. (The bigger end of the almond should be pressed into the candy). Place on chip bag.

Dip the pumpkins into the chocolate. Set aside on chip bag for chocolate to harden.

Serves: 6

JUST A THOUGHT: All that we are is a result of what we have thought. Buddha

---

New Year's Party Time Snack Mix

1 bag Corn chips	1 packet Lemon Cool-down
1 packet Chili soup seasoning	2 packages Hot peanuts
2 packages Peanuts	1 M&Ms plain candies
1 M&Ms peanut candies	3 packages Energizer nut mix
1 package Sunflower seeds	

In 2 large chip bags, divide all ingredients equally and mix together. Watch the Rose Bowl with friend. **Enjoy!**

Serves: 8

> **JUST A THOUGHT:** A flower is the most eligible object in the world. Unknown

St. Patrick's Clover Cake

All Holiday's Basic Cookie/Cake recipe	1 All Holiday's Basic Frosting recipe
1 M&M candies (green only)	Water

On a large chip bag, shape the dough into a 4-leaf clover. Heat the frosting in the hot pot while shaping clover.

In about a teaspoon of water, add the green M&Ms to remove color. Add the colored water to the frosting and mix well. Spread over cake. Eat the rest of the M&Ms.

Serves: 6

TOPPING IDEAS: Sprinkle crushed mint sticks, fruit sticks, more green M&Ms, or crushed Fireballs on top of frosting before it sets.

> **JUST A THOUGHT:** If we want to change a situation, we first have to change ourselves. And to change ourselves effectively, we first have to change our perceptions. Stephen R. Covey

Thanksgiving Turkey

1 package Oatmeal cookies	1 package Candy corn
2 Hershey's plain candy bars	1 M&Ms plain candies
1 package Orange slices (cut in half lengthwise)	

Place cookies on an empty chip bag. Leave candy bars in wrappers and melt in hot pot. Cut 32 orange slices in half, lengthwise. These will be the wings.

Cut a little corner off the chocolate wrappers to squeeze chocolate. Adhere the beak (candy corn), the eyes (M&Ms), and the orange slices (wings) with the Hershey's candy bar. **Gobble! Gobble!**

Serves: 32 Cookies

VARIATION: Macaroon cookies can easily replace the Oatmeal cookies. The turkey will just be a lighter color.

JUST A THOUGHT: Worry is like a rocking chair. It gives you something to do, but doesn't get you anywhere. Amy Jones

Valentine Hearts

1 package Pasqual candies (separate colors)

After deciding what color heart you want, slam the candies on the concrete floor to break up (leave in wrapper). Take out of wrapper and drop into insert cup. Heat until the candies are soft and pliable.

Then, place in a small chip bag or tortilla bag. The tortilla bag is the better choice because it's more pliable. It's best to use one corner in the bottom of the bag to start the bottom of the heart. Keep adding candies as you continue to shape it into a heart. Leave the candies in the insert cup in the hot pot so they remain warm while you are adding the candies. **It's Charming!**

Serves: 1

VARIATION: Try using different colors and make each color a thin stripe. You can mold the candy into various shapes for other holiday's, too!

JUST A THOUGHT: One of the hardest things to learn in life is which bridge to cross and which bridge to burn. Unknown

Wedding Cake

2 packages Vanilla cream cookies	8 packets Cream cheese
2 packages Chocolate cream cookies	1 package Chocolate covered peanuts
¼ bottle Strawberry preserves	1 Hershey's plain candy bar
1 tablespoon Peanut butter	6 Chick-O-Sticks (crushed)
Water	

Bottom layer (square): Separate cream filling from 2 packages of chocolate cookies. In a large bowl, crush cookies. Add a little water and mix well (until it is a moist but firm dough). Transfer to a large chip bag. Add the chocolate peanuts and mix well. Cook in hot pot for about 30 minutes. Take out and mix well. Form into a square on a chip bag. In the same cookie bag, add the filling, 2 cream cheese, and Hershey's. Melt and mix well. Spread over cake.

Middle layer (triangle): Separate cream filling from Peanut Butter cookies. In a large bowl, crush cookies and add a little water to form dough. Add 1 tablespoon of peanut butter. Stir in the Chick-O-Sticks and mix well. Transfer to a cooking bag. Cook for 30 minutes. Take out and mix well. Shape into a triangle and place on top of square. In an insert cup, add the filling and 2 cream cheese. Melt and mix well. Spread over cake.

Top layer (circle): Separate cream filling from vanilla cookies. In a large bowl, crush cookies. Add enough water to form into dough. Divide in half. Form the first one into a circle, and place on top of the triangle. Mix jam and 2 cream cheese packs until well blended. Spread over cake. Form other half into same size circle and place on top. In an insert cup, add filling and 2 cream cheese. Melt and mix thoroughly. Spread over top layer.

Serves: 18

VARIATION: Decorate layers with crushed M&Ms, Chick-O-Sticks, mint sticks, or fruit sticks. Add a Snickers, Milky Way, or Butterfinger in place of the Chick-O-Sticks in the triangle.

JUST A THOUGHT: You are not on this journey by chance, but for a special purpose. Clifford Goldstein

---

V
Beverage Treats

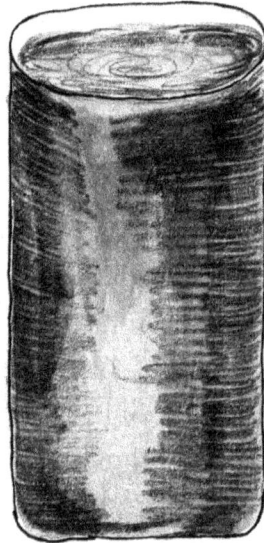
Just Peachy

Cappuccino

Coffee

Better Tea

1 can Lemon tea	1 can Sprite

Divide equally into 2 insert cups. Stir well and enjoy your special tea.
Serves: 2

> **DID YOU KNOW?** It takes just 40 days for most Americans to earn enough money to pay for their food supply for the entire year. In comparison with the 129 days it takes the average American to earn enough money to pay federal, state, and local taxes for the year.

Butterscotch Coffee

1 teaspoon Instant coffee	2-3 Butterscotch candies (crushed)
2 packets Sweeteners	Water

In an insert cup, fill with 1 cup of water and add the candies. Heat in hot pot until candy is dissolved. Pour into mug and add coffee and sweeteners. Stir well.
Yum!
Serves: 1

> **DID YOU KNOW?** Baskin-Robbins introduced the new flavor "Lunar Cheesecake" to commemorate America's landing on the moon on July 20, 1969.

Chocolate Coffee Swirl

1 pint Vanilla ice cream	2 teaspoons Instant coffee
Hot water	Chocolate syrup (to taste)

In 2 mugs, place 1 teaspoon of coffee in each mug. Mix coffee with water and add chocolate syrup. Gently mix the ice cream into the coffee. **Enjoy!**
Serves: 2

> **DID YOU KNOW?** Egg white is the common name for the clear liquid (also called albumin/albumen or glair) contained within an egg. It is the cytoplasm of the egg, which until fertilization is a single cell. It consists mainly of about 10 percent proteins dissolved in water. Its primary purpose is to protect the egg yolk and also to provide additional nutrition for the growth of the embryo, as it is rich in proteins and is of high nutritional value. Unlike the egg yolk, it contains little fat.

Chocolate Drink Mix on the "Ready"

1 bag Hot chocolate drink mix	½ bag Instant coffee
10 Mint sticks (crushed)	Water
2 bags Dry milk	

Thoroughly crush mint sticks. Pour everything into a large bowl and mix until blended together. Then, return to the hot chocolate bag. This is an excellent mix to keep on hand. I make a funnel with a magazine page for easier pouring.

Serves: Varied

DID YOU KNOW? Actually a fruit, it took a ruling by the Supreme Court in 1893 to make a tomato a vegetable. This is our tax dollars at work.

Chocolatier Hot Chocolate

1 tablespoon Dry milk	1 packet Sweetener
3 tablespoons Hot chocolate drink mix	Water
1 Milky Way candy bar	

Use ½ Milky Way for this recipe. In an insert cup, combine all ingredients with enough hot water and stir until candy bar is melted. Make 2 and share with a friend!

Serves: 1

DID YOU KNOW? Peanuts are salted in the shell by boiling them in a heavily salted solution, then allowing them to dry.

Creamy Hot Chocolate

3 teaspoons Hot chocolate drink mix	2 packets Sweeteners
½ package Vanilla cappuccino	Water
1 teaspoon Dry milk	

In a mug, fill with hot water and add all the ingredients. Stir well.
Relax and Savor!
Serves: 1

DID YOU KNOW? Quality dark chocolate contains flavonoids which help reduce the risk of heart disease.

Desheon's Tea Pot

2 Tea bags	½ packet Orange sports drink
½ Fruit stick (crushed)	1 packet Sweetener
Water	

In an insert cup, combine all ingredients and stir until fruit stick is dissolved. Serve hot or cold.

Serves: 1

DID YOU KNOW? A toaster uses almost half as much energy as a full-sized oven.

Faux Black Russian

1 cup Hot chocolate	1 can Coca-Cola

Prepare hot chocolate to drink. Let cool completely. In 2 insert cups, divide equally and add cola. Stir well. Delicious! Even better if you can mix with ice!

Serves: 2

DID YOU KNOW? If you shake a can of mixed nuts, the larger ones will rise to the top.

Faux Latté

1 package Irish Cream cappuccino	½ package Vanilla cappuccino
3 teaspoons Dry milk	1 packet Sweetener
Water	

Combine in cup with hot water and stir well. **Enjoy!**

Serves:1

VARIATION: If you need caffeine, or just want more of a coffee flavor, stir in a teaspoonful of instant coffee.

Faux Strawberry Margarita

2 cans Strawberry soda	10 packets Lemon-lime sports drink

Wash out a large chip bag. Double bag before you mix everything together. Have someone hold bags while you pour everything in. Stir well.

Carefully pour back into cans. **Cheers!**

Serves: 2

Firey Tea

1 Tea bag	1 packet Lemon Cool-down
2 Fireballs jaw breakers (broken in pieces)	Water
2 packets Sweeteners	

In an insert cup, fill with water and add tea bag and fireballs. Heat in hot pot until the fireballs have dissolved. Remove the tea bag and add the Cool-down and sweeteners. Mix well. **Sit back and relax!**

Serves: 1

> **DID YOU KNOW?** When Swiss cheese ferments, a bacterial action generates gas. As the gas is liberated, it bubbles through the cheese leaving holes. Cheese makers call them "eyes."

Fruity Lime Drink

1 Fruit stick (crush fine)	2 packets Sweeteners
1 Water bottle w/water	1 packet Lemon-lime sports drink

In your hot pot insert, fill with about 1 inch of water. Pour crushed fruit stick in and heat until it's dissolved. Keep stirring. When it's dissolved, cool it by holding cup under cold water.

Fill water bottle ½ full with cold water. Pour in fruit stick water. Then, shake for a minute. Add remaining ingredients. Fill the rest of the way with cold water. **Shake and enjoy!**

Serves: 1

> **DID YOU KNOW?** By recycling just one glass bottle, the amount of energy that is being saved is enough to light a 100 watt bulb for four hours.

Grape Slushie

3 Rainbow Freezes	1 can Grape soda

Divide the 3 freezes and the soda equally into 2 insert cups. Stir well.
Serves: 2

SUBSTITUTE: Any flavor of soda will work. For a less sweet taste you can use a strawberry soda or Sprite. Or use a Big Red or Big Blue for a sweeter taste.

> **DID YOU KNOW?** The inventor of the Waffle Iron did not like waffles.

Hot Toddy

2 Fireballs jaw breakers (broken in pieces)	1 packet Lemon Cool-down
2 packets Sweeteners	Water

In an insert cup, fill with 1 cup of water and add the fireballs. Heat in hot pot until completely dissolved. Add the Cool-down and sweeteners and mix well. **Enjoy!**
Serves: 1

☺ **HEALTHFUL HINT!**:.If you have a cold or fever, then stir in 2 CTM's and go to sleep…a sure cure for what ails you! **Zzzzz…..**

> **DID YOU KNOW?** Eggs will age more in one day at room temperature than they will in one week in the refrigerator.

Lemon-Mint Tea

1 Tea bag	2 packets Sweeteners
½ Mint stick (crushed)	1 packet Lemon Cool-down

In an insert cup, fill with water and add tea bag and mint stick. Heat in hot pot until dissolved. Then, add the sweeteners and Cool-down and stir.
Refreshing!
Serves: 1

> **DID YOU KNOW?**   The water buffalo's milk is used to make authentic Italian mozzarella cheese.

Luck of the Irish Coffee

1 teaspoon Instant coffee	1 package Irish Cream cappuccino
2 tablespoons Chocolate syrup	2 packets Sweeteners
Water	

Combine all ingredients in a mug, add hot water and stir until combined. **Relax and enjoy!**
Serves: 1

SUBSTITUTE: 1 heaping tablespoon of hot chocolate drink mix can be used in place of the chocolate syrup. Add a teaspoon of crushed mint stick or a crushed cinnamon stick for an added flavor that will make you want seconds!

Mint Coffee

1 teaspoon Instant coffee	1-2 packets Sweeteners
½ Mint stick (crushed)	Water

Fill mug with hot water and add the coffee, sweeteners, and mint stick. Stir well.
It's soothing!
Serves: 1

DID YOU KNOW? In 1926, when a Los Angeles restaurant owner with the All-American name of Bob Cobb was looking for a way to use up leftovers, he threw together some avacado, celery, tomato, chives, watermelon, hard-boiled eggs, chicken, bacon, and Roquefort cheese, and named it after himself — Cobb Salad

Minty Hot Chocolate

3 teaspoons Hot chocolate drink mix	2 packets Sweeteners
½ Mint stick (crushed)	Water

In an insert cup, fill with 1½ cups of water and the mint stick. Heat in hot pot until completely dissolved. Add remaining ingredients and stir well.
Serves: 1

SUBSTITUTE: A cinnamon stick or Fireballs jaw breaker can be used in addition to, or in place of the mint stick.

DID YOU KNOW? The difference between apple juice and apple cider is the apple juice is the juice of the fruit only. And, apple cider is the whole apple—skins, seeds, all—which give it the fuller body and deeper color. The juice is pasteurized and the cider is not.

New Year's Champagne

1 can Sprite	1 can Cranberry juice

Chill cans and then divide equally into 2 insert cups. Mix well. **Toast away!!!**
Serves: 2

DID YOU KNOW? Worcestershire sauce, the popular English sauce, is made from dissolved anchovies. The anchovies are soaked in vinegar until they have completely melted. The sauce contains the bones and all.

Orange Tart

1 can Fanta Orange	1 packet Lemon-Cool down

Combine both and stir well. Enjoy! With ice, it's even better.
Serves: 1

> **DID YOU KNOW?** The plant pigment that gives carrots and other vegetables their vivid orange color is Beta-Carotene. Fruits and vegetables that are yellow/orange in color contain Beta-Carotene and carrots are one of the richest in this nutrient. Our bodies convert Beta-Carotene into Vitamin A.

Party Punch

3 Sherbet Push-ups	2 Rainbow Freeze's
1 can Orange/Pineapple juice	

Divide everything equally into 2 cups. Mix together and enjoy!
Serves: 2

> **DID YOU KNOW?** The daughter of confectioner Lee Hirschfield is commemorated in the name of the sweet he invented: Although his daughter's real name was Clara, she went by the nickname Tootsie, and in her honor, her doting father named his chewy chocolate logs Tootsie rolls.

Plain ol' Tea

1 Water bottle (empty)	7 Tea bags
3 Fireballs jaw breakers (crushed)	1 packet Sweetener
1 packet Lemon Cool-down	Hot water

Heat water until hot. Remove wrappers from fireballs and add into an empty mug. Place tea bags into the mug and add water to the rim. Allow the tea to sit and simmer for 20 minutes.

After 20 minutes, remove tea bags and stir lightly. Pour 2 ounces of tea into empty water bottle. Add 1 lemon Cool-down. Add one sweetener and apply cap tightly to tea bottle and shake. Remove cap from bottle. Fill bottle to rim with cold water. Replace cap and shake again. Enjoy!
Serves: 1

> **DID YOU KNOW?** Watermelon is grown in over 96 countries. Over 1,200 varieties of watermelon are grown worldwide with about 200 variations of watermelons in the U.S.

Sangrarita

1 can Coca-Cola	1 can Grape soda
1 packet Grape Cool-down	

Divide equally into 2 insert cups and stir well. Try to find some ice – its even better!
Serves: 2

DID YOU KNOW? The Agen plum, which would become the basis of the U.S. prune industry, was first planted in California in 1856.

Tangy Twist

1 packet Grape Cool-down	1 packet Lemon Cool-down
1 packet Orange sports drink	1 can Sprite

Pour into an insert cup and mix everything together. Add a little water for your preferred taste. **Tart and Good!**
Serves: 1

DID YOU KNOW? Decaffeinated coffee is not 100% caffeine free. When coffee is being decaffeinated, 2% of the caffeine still remains in it.

Tart Fizzle

1 can Sprite	1 packet Orange sports drink
1 packet Grape Cool-down	

Combine everything and mix well. **Wonderfully tart!**
Serves: 1

DID YOU KNOW? Pringles aren't actually potato chips. Despite this, they were originally called "Pringles New Fangled Potato Chips." However, they only contain about 42 percent potato based content, with most of the rest being from wheat starch and various types of flour, including from corn and rice. The U. S. Food and Drug Administration made them change the name because their product didn't technically meet the definition of a potato chip. Further, they were only allowed to use the word "chip" in very restrictive ways. This resulted in them changing the name to include "potato crisps," rather than "chips." Funny enough, changing it to "crisps" ultimately got them into the same type of trouble in the United Kingdom.

Books For Sale

Wounded Bird by Nancy Hall, is about Celeste Johnson's justice by terror in Texas after her husband was murdered. Wrongly convicted of conspiring with her husband's confessed murderer, Celeste's story is a must read for anyone wanting to understand how an innocent person gets trapped in the nightmare of being falsely accused and prosecuted for a crime he or she didn't commit. Includes letters from Gatesville Prison between Celeste and her mother Nancy Hall.
184 pages, softcover.

$14.99

Order with a credit card from
www.authorhouse.com/bookstore
To locate the book enter **Wounded Bird** or **Nancy Hall** in the search box.

Trial By Perjury: Millionaire, Mania & Misinformation By Nancy Hall

Celeste Beard Johnson was convicted in 2003 of capital murder in the death of her then husband Steven F. Beard, who died of natural causes in 2000. She was sentenced to life in prison. Nancy Hall cites extensively from the case record to explain how the the prosecution was able to convince the jury that Steven Beard's death was murder and that Celeste was involved in his shooting.
252 pages. Kindle e-book.

$4.99

Order with a credit card from

www.amazon.com
To locate the book enter **Trial By Perjury** or **Nancy Hall** in the search box.

Books published by The Justice Institute

From The Big House To Your House

By Ceyma Bina, Tina Cornelius, Barbara Holder, Celeste Johnson, Trenda Kemmerer, and Louanne Larson

Includes 200 recipes for easy to prepare meals, snacks and desserts. *From The Big House To Your House* has two hundred easy to prepare recipes for meals, snacks and desserts. Written by six women imprisoned in Texas, the recipes can be made from basic items a prisoner can purchase from their commissary, or people on the outside can purchase from a convenience or grocery store. Also included are many cost saving tips.

$14 (postage paid to U.S. mailing address)
132 pages, softcover

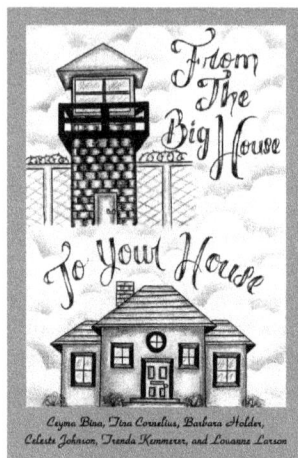

Edwin M. Borchard - Convicting The Innocent and State Indemnity For Errors Of Criminal Justice

Compiled and Introduction by Hans Sherrer

Convicting the Innocent has not lost its luster as one of the most insightful books published on the topic of wrongful convictions. Seventy-one years after its publication the multitude of causes underlying the cases of injustice it details not only continue to plague the legal system in the United States, but they are arguably more prevalent today than when the book was published. Also included is Borchard's seminal article that pointed the way in this country for compensation for persons exonerated of their convicted crimes: *European Systems Of State Indemnity For Errors of Criminal Justice*.

$21.95 (postage paid to U.S. mailing address)
358 pages, softcover

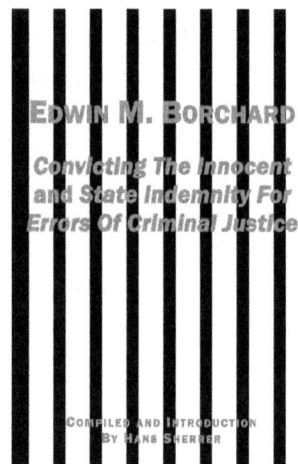

Kirstin Blaise Lobato vs. State Of Nevada

Compiled by Hans Sherrer & Michelle Ravell

Complete 770-page Nevada state habeas corpus petition filed with the Clark County District Court in Las Vegas on May 5, 2010. The petition's 79 grounds include 24 new evidence grounds; 2 *Brady* violation grounds; 52 ineffective assistance of counsel grounds; and 1 actual innocence ground. Included is a complete index of the petition to easily find each page referring to a particular topic.

Each ground is explained and supported by documentation and exhibits that include reports by forensic science, medical and entomology experts.

$20 (postage paid to U.S. mailing address)
792 pages, softcover

Kirstin Blaise Lobato's Unreasonable Conviction – Revised and Updated Second Edition
By Hans Sherrer

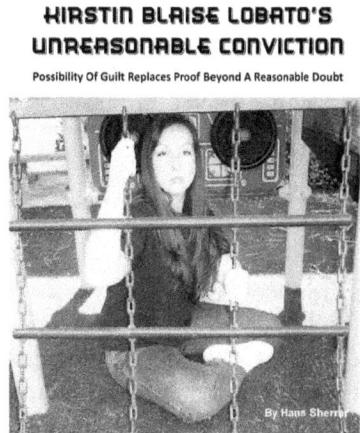

KIRSTIN BLAISE LOBATO'S UNREASONABLE CONVICTION

Possibility Of Guilt Replaces Proof Beyond A Reasonable Doubt

By Hans Sherrer

Kirstin Blaise Lobato was convicted and imprisoned for the July 2001 murder of a homeless man in Las Vegas, even though:

- There is no forensic, physical, eyewitness or confession evidence that either the 18-year-old Kirstin or her bright red car was at the murder scene, while fingerprints, DNA evidence and bloody shoeprints leading away from the body exclude her.
- On the day of the murder eleven alibi witnesses saw or talked with her in Panaca where she was living 170 miles north of Las Vegas.
- There is no evidence she or her car was in Las Vegas on the day of the murder.
- She was arrested based on third-hand gossip without any police investigation.

This revised and updated second edition includes information through September 2010, including a summary of Ms. Lobato's Nevada habeas petition that includes 24 grounds based on new evidence of her actual innocence.

Written by Hans Sherrer, editor and publisher of *Justice:Denied* magazine.

$12 (postage paid to U.S. mailing address)
174 pages, softcover

Dehumanization Is Not An Option
By Hans Sherrer

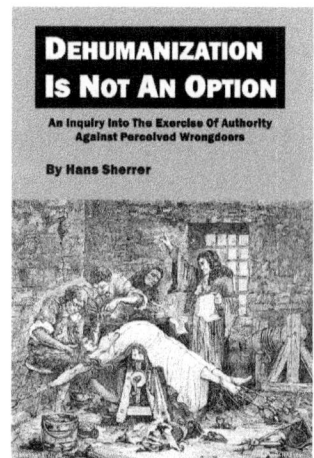

DEHUMANIZATION IS NOT AN OPTION

An Inquiry Into The Exercise Of Authority Against Perceived Wrongdoers

By Hans Sherrer

People around the world were shocked when gruesome details were revealed about the mistreatment of prisoners at Abu Ghraib, Guantanamo Bay and other detention facilities run by the United States. Yet their treatment in general differs only by degree from the treatment of people imprisoned in the U.S. and other countries.

This mistreatment is not due to the rogue actions of a few "bad apples." It is a predictable response by people placed in a position of authority over those they see as undeserving of humane treatment.

Dehumanization Is Not An Option explores how the inhumane treatment of real or suspected wrongdoers is contributed to by the unleashing of authoritarian attitudes, and that bureaucratic systems contribute to barbaric behavior.

Chapters include:
- Obedience To Authority Is Endemic
- Dehumanization Paves The Path To Mistreatment
- Psychological Dehumanization of Prisoners
- Bureaucracies Fuel Dehumanization

Written by Hans Sherrer, editor and publisher of *Justice:Denied* magazine.

$10 (postage paid to U.S. mailing address)

100 pages, softcover

Phantom Spies, Phantom Justice
By Miriam Moskowitz

The human cost of the anti-Communist witch-hunt during the McCarthy era is brought to life in *Phantom Spies: Phantom Justice* – Miriam Moskowitz' personal account of that terrible time. Ms. Moskowitz' was arrested in 1950 and prosecuted for conspiracy to obstruct justice during a grand jury investigation of suspected Soviet espionage. She was sensationally branded by the prosecution and in news stories as part of an atom bomb spy ring. Yet it was a lie. *Phantom Spies: Phantom Justice* reveals through Ms. Moskowitz' many years of diligent research of court records, FBI documents and other sources that her prosecutors knew she was innocent, and yet kept silent as the lone witness against her repeatedly lied during his testimony. Now in her late-90s, Ms. Moskowitz has lived for 62 years with the false stigma of being a convicted felon and an enemy of the United States. Michael Meeropol, older son of Ethel and Julius Rosenberg writes about *Phantom Spies: Phantom Justice*: "Miriam Moskowitz' story about how she became "collateral damage" in the government's pursuit of real and fake spies is a must reading for all who cherish our constitutional form of government."

$24.95 (postage paid to U.S. mailing address)
289 pages, softcover

TO ORDER any of these books send a check or money order with complete mailing information to:

Justice Denied
PO Box 66291
Seattle, WA 98166

Or order with a credit card from: **www.justicedenied.org/books.html**

A catalog of dozens of books related to wrongful convictions, and legal and educational self-help that are sold by Justice Denied is available by writing:

Justice Denied
PO Box 66291
Seattle, WA 98166

Celeste Beard Johnson vs. The State of Texas

Trial by Perjury by Nancy Hall (Celeste's mother) is a new Kindle e-book on Amazon.com that is based on Celeste's trial court transcripts. Information about *Trial by Perjury* is at, www.tinyurl.com/n7k4p4p.

On October 2, 1999, Tracey Tarlton shot Steven Beard (Celeste's husband) with a 20-gauge shotgun while he was sleeping in his bed. The wound was not fatal.

Tarlton and Celeste had been friends for about six months, but prior to the shooting Steven and Celeste had agreed to terminate all relationships with Tarlton because of her bizarre attachment to Celeste.

Almost four months after the shooting Steven died in 2000, and his autopsy concluded his cause of death was pulmonary embolism. The shooting had nothing to do with Steven's illness or his death.

An embolism occurs when an artery in your lungs becomes blocked. Most clots originate in your legs but they can also form in arm veins. Once you've had one pulmonary embolism, you're at increased risk of more, and many of these recurrences can be fatal. The most common symptoms are breathlessness when you exert yourself and general fatigue, fainting, dizziness, swollen legs or ankles, and pressure or pain in your chest is also common when pulmonary hypertension becomes severe. Steven Beard suffered all these symptoms the last year of his life. He was in the hospital two times in September 1999 with dizziness and fainting – which was prior to the shooting.

Although Steven Beard died of natural causes the District Attorney's Office tricked Tracey Tarlton into believing his death was caused by the unrelated shooting. In exchange for a reduced charge and sentence of 20 years in prison Tarlton manufactured a story that Celeste had conspired to kill Steven for financial gain.

Relying on Tarlton's confession the DA's office prosecuted Celeste for murder on the basis his death was a consequence of the shooting. Celeste denied having any involvement in Tarlton's actions, and during her trial in 2003 she presented expert medical testimony that Steven died from natural causes. Nevertheless, the jury convicted her of murder and she was sentenced to life in prison with eligibility for parole after 40 years.

Tarlton was paroled in 2011, while Celeste remains imprisoned for a crime that didn't occur because there was no murder. Celeste vehemently asserts she is unjustly imprisoned.

Information about Celeste's case is online at: http://www.celestebeardneedshelp.com.
Celeste would like to hear from you so write:
Celeste Johnson 1157250
Mt. View Unit
2305 Ransom Road
Gatesville, TX 76528
celestebj11@gmail.com

www.ingramcontent.com/pod-product-compliance
Lightning Source LLC
LaVergne TN
LVHW061226060426
835509LV00012B/1444